FOLLOW
YOUR

DEBBIE TIMMS

ISBN 978-1-64299-443-8 (paperback)
ISBN 978-1-64299-643-2 (hardcover)
ISBN 978-1-64299-444-5 (digital)

Christian Faith Publishing, Inc.
832 Park Avenue
Meadville, PA 16335
www.christianfaithpublishing.com

Printed in the United States of America

Prologue

It was a beautiful spring day in Prescott. Everything about the day was ordinary, and if it had been any other day, I wouldn't have remembered a single detail, but this day would prove to be far from ordinary. I clearly remember everything about that day. Arizona has the most beautiful blue skies, and that day was no exception. It was spring, and flowers were blooming everywhere. We had been out doing our usual Saturday morning activities, breakfast at our favorite eatery and running errands. My son, Davey, and I had been texting back and forth that morning, but we did not speak. Something that has haunted me ever since. He was being funny and was excited about his plans for the day, and I was just enjoying those texts.

The call that every parent dreads came just before midnight.

I want to tell you my story—the story of my son, Davey, and my journey to survive his death.

The loss of a child at any age may be one of the most difficult things there is in life with which to deal. I want to tell my story so that maybe I can help other grieving parents survive something this horrific and reassure them that the human spirit can triumph over circumstances that seem unbearable. I have learned so much along the way. I want to share Davey's life and his experiences, what those experiences have taught me, and how I have survived. I want to share my journey into what I have learned about the afterlife and what an important part of my story it is.

I want you to know that, even in my deepest grief, I knew Davey was all around me and looking out for me, for all of us. Even then, I wanted to make him proud.

CHAPTER

1

I was a twenty-seven-year-old nurse, married, with a four-year-old daughter, named Cari, when Davey came roaring into the world. I remember thinking that I couldn't believe this beautiful baby boy belonged to me. I know, just about all moms say that, right? But I had had such a horrible pregnancy (picture nine months of vomiting, IVs for dehydration, and the most god-awful heartburn in the universe) that I was truly shocked that he was so healthy and beautiful. When one spends the majority of her pregnancy feasting on cherry Rolaids, well, I thought he might actually look like one when he came out!

We decided to name him David Anthony. Looking back, nobody ever really called him David except his teachers and coaches. Cari and I always called him Davey, and his dad, from day one, called him Bubba. His friends always referred to him by his last name, Compton. I remember once asking my mom why she referred to the now-teenaged Davey as Dave. She said, "Have you seen the size of that kid?" Just because he was 6'4" when entering high school! To his sister and me, he was always and still is just our Davey.

His first six months were difficult, to say the least. I had gone back to work after six weeks. I had a daughter to care for, and Davey decided he would be colicky. At night. Every night. There wasn't a lot of sleeping for either of us. But you know what? I truly think that was the time that we really began to bond. We spent a lot of one-on-one time during those late-night/early-morning hours. I won't lie. I always felt terrible that I could not make him feel any better. Walking him for hours was the only thing that helped. I wanted to pull out my hair many times; frustration coupled with exhaustion is a terrible way to feel.

When Davey was six months old, I took him to the pediatrician for his regular six-month checkup. He passed with flying colors. Me, on the other hand, not so much. Dr. Burgett took one look at me, and we had a nice chat. By nice chat, I mean she told me that it was time for my little Davey to teach himself how to fall asleep. I wasn't doing him or myself any favors by not ever letting him cry. I was sent home with instructions for his bedtime that night. No picking up, no matter what, he had to figure it out. I was only allowed to rub his tummy. Boy, was I terrified! Listening to a baby cry is torture. He cried for twenty minutes and then slept all night. The next morning, both my husband and I were reluctant to go in and check on him. We walked in, and my sweet baby was sitting there quietly in his crib. Who knew? From then on, he pretty much slept every night. It was a miracle!

From the time Davey was a little boy, he was pretty much attached to my hip. He used to love to wrap his little fist around my "yellow" hair. He would regularly announce to the world that he was going to marry a girl with "yellow hair" when he was bigger.

He was a little shy and awkward as a young boy in social situations—except when it came to asking questions. He was so inquisitive and wanted to know about everything. He would ask people questions all the time, whether it was appropriate or not, in that straightforward, uninhibited way that children usually have. Once we were in line at McDonald's, and he walked up to a rather tall lady and asked her point-blank, "Why are you so big?" Yikes! I wanted to disappear into the floor! I remember wondering at times if he was ever going to stop asking so many questions. You know, he never did stop. What I wouldn't give to hear one of those questions now.

I remember his first day of preschool. He was terrified, and I was so upset having to leave him. I had already been through it with Cari. I should have been a pro, right? Wrong. He was wrapped around my leg so tight, I thought I might have to detach said leg so I could get to work.

He was a little on the shy side through most of his childhood, something he inherited from me. Cari was the complete opposite and wasn't too alarmed about anything as a child. She was always happy and outgoing. She was more like her dad, and Davey was all me.

Davey's dad and I married at a relatively young age, and it's safe to say it was a complicated relationship from the get-go, but it wasn't always difficult, and we did have some happy years. We spent the first several years buying and renovating two homes and having babies. We also worked full-time. Once both kids started school, I went to work part-time. When they were in school, I worked. I was able to pick them up from school and be there for them when they were home. Once I went part-time, my husband began to work more hours. We continued this way for several years, living life and raising a family. Even so, our troubles were always lurking, and after twenty-one years of marriage, we decided to divorce.

Although Davey's dad was gone a lot, Davey idolized him. His dad was a master mechanic who could do just about anything with his hands. There just wasn't anything he couldn't fix. I think that's where Davey discovered his passion for tearing things apart, fixing them, and putting them back together. Like a puppy, he would follow him outside into the garage. He wanted to be just like his dad. As he got older, I think his dad's absences were harder on him.

As Davey reached the middle-school years, he gained some weight, as what often happens with adolescents. He was what one would call chunky. Poor kid also inherited my bad eyesight and wore braces. I think it's safe to say those issues can be difficult for middle-schoolers, and I believe that is when he started to develop body-image issues. He was also quite a bit taller than all his friends were. He became uncomfortable in his own skin. It took him a long time to come to terms with those things. By the time he stopped growing, he was 6'6" tall!

Even in those years, as he was struggling with those issues, he grew into the kindest, most polite and was an ever-still-inquisitive young man. Boy, did he love to learn. He just wasn't all that comfortable in the classroom. The things that excited him were things he learned outside the classroom. Working with his hands, discovering how things were built. His preferred methods of learning were to touch, see, and feel the problem so that he could properly solve it. He adored anything and everything related to cars and speed. Both his dad and I grew up around stock-car racing, so it's understandable that he inherited the love that we have for racing. He just couldn't get enough. He wanted to learn everything. He would follow his dad around like a puppy when he was outside working on cars. His dad wanted him to watch and learn, and Davey just wanted to do. It caused a scuffle or two. Eventually, his dad purchased a race truck to run at one of the local tracks. Davey wanted to drive that thing something fierce, but his dad just didn't think Davey was ready. He never did get the chance to drive the truck. After a couple of seasons, the racetrack shut its doors, and the truck was sold.

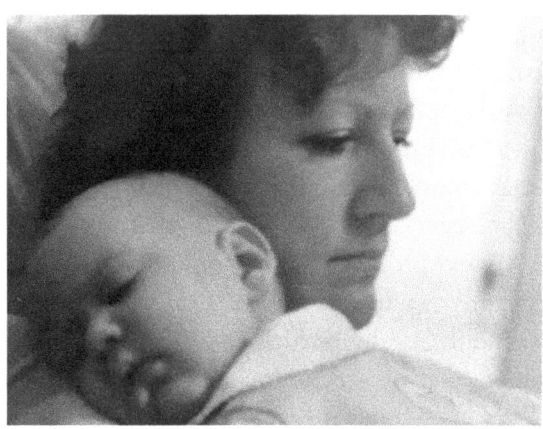

As he got older, he purchased his dream car, an older Toyota Supra. I saw that car and thought to myself, *Yikes.* It wasn't pretty. Because I wanted to stay on Davey's good side, I didn't say that out loud. He rebuilt that car from the ground up, and when it was finished, it was a thing of beauty. He loved that car. He made a comment once that he would be OK if he died in that car; that was how much he loved it. We couldn't possibly have foreseen the irony in his statement.

He also loved dogs. We always had at least one dog while the kids were growing up. The two dogs that stole his heart were Mandi and Maggie. He used to always tell me he wished he could clone Maggie; he just loved her so much. He would say she was just the perfect dog. They have a bond that continues to this day. You see, three months after Davey's accident, Maggie became ill. The vet could find nothing wrong with her; she just stopped eating and drinking. She was only six years old. It was so hard for Davey's dad, but she did not improve and had to be put down. I have believed since it happened that she died of a broken heart and needed to be with Davey. I completely understand how she felt.

When Davey was about to enter high school, we decided to talk to him about trying out for the football team. We thought his size would be an asset to the team and it would be good for him to be a part of something, especially during the difficult high school years. He agreed, and so off to tryouts he went. When he walked onto the field, the coaches thought they had died and gone to heaven! This kid was going to be their offensive line. He made the freshman team. It soon became apparent, however, that Davey was just too nice. He was not aggressive on the field at all. No matter what they tried, Davey remained nice and calm. I remember thinking that, if the worst thing that someone can say about your kid is that he is "just too nice," well, I can certainly live with that. While he didn't get much playing time, his decision to try out and be a part of that team changed everything for him. Football is a pretty big deal where he went to high school. Suddenly, his size was a good thing. He no longer felt ostracized, and he was no longer the biggest kid around. Not only did he learn the game of football; he learned so many important life lessons, things that carried him throughout the rest of his life. Things like hard work, discipline, achieving goals, integrity, and loyalty.

He was close to a lot of the guys on the team throughout high school and well after graduation. Then there were others whose friendships fell by the wayside. He had been so sure that, because of the things they had been through as a team, they would remain close forever. He used to tell me that, while he was sometimes sad at the loss of some of those friendships, those were the people who introduced him to what would become his "crew" and his best friend, Brian.

There were other challenges in high school as well. Then, as now, there was a lot of drug use. Even though as a parent you know those things go on, it's always hard to hear it when it could involve your child. Davey's dad made it clear to both kids that drug use would not be tolerated, and for whatever reason, it got through to both of them. We were lucky, I know. Did either of them ever experiment with marijuana? Years later, I learned that they both tried it but weren't all that interested in doing it.

Years before, I had decided that I wanted them to go to school in Orange County. It was a lot of work to get them into that district, and finally, it was allowed because my job was in the OC. It was a smaller, much-better school district than was the one where we lived. A lot of the kids came from affluent families. Davey used to wonder out loud why kids who were afforded so many opportunities would resort to drugs and other activities that could ruin their lives. During our marriage, we were strictly middle class. We both worked and provided for our kids, but Davey would not be driving a BMW to work like some of his classmates did. He drove in every day in his very-well-used Toyota Cressida, and he loved that car!

With all the issues he faced in high school, I used to worry endlessly about him. He had body issues and normal teenage angst. By the time he started high school, Davey's dad and I had already divorced. I just felt it was a lot for a kid to handle. Cari had recently graduated and was enrolled in college nearby. I had more time for Davey, and I was able to spend a lot of time talking to him, even when he didn't want to have those conversations. As he got older, he was less and less interested in having heart-to-heart talks with me. I was a mom, for cripe's sake; I didn't actually *know* anything! Even so, I kept the conversations going. Cari was always close by, and even though everyone was busy, the three of us maintained our close relationship, and that never changed. Luckily, they both made it through the teenage years relatively unscathed.

CHAPTER

2

As I have mentioned previously, my tumultuous marriage finally came to a heartbreaking end when Cari was seventeen and Davey was thirteen. It was painful for all of us. I tried to do the right things for the kids. We spent a lot of time talking about it, and I took them to a family therapist. There is not one party totally responsible when a marriage fails, and I will forever carry guilt that these precious babies were subjected to any of it. They deserved better.

There were many challenges, the most painful being when the judge said that, because the kids were older, they could choose which parent they wanted to live with. Cari chose me, and Davey decided to live with his dad. He thought this would be a chance for them to become closer, and he didn't want his dad to be alone. Was it difficult? You bet it was! I was devastated by the fact that our family was fractured beyond repair.

There were practical problems that had to be addressed, for example, I had to find a place to live. For someone who had never lived alone, the prospect was daunting. Everything was changing, and feeling overwhelmed, I decided to move in with my parents for a few months until I could figure everything out. By the time that happened, Cari had graduated and had decided to get an apartment with her best friend. That was hard for me too. I spent a lot of time beating myself up, thinking she wouldn't have moved out if not for the divorce.

I'll spare you the details of what happened and why; it will suffice to say we all carried scars that took a long time to heal.

Even though Davey was living with his dad, I moved only five minutes away. I still picked him up every morning and took him to school and picked him up in the afternoon until he learned to drive. I still went to every event, doctor's appointment, everything. I saw him every day. The only difference was that we did not live together.

Years later, Davey and I were having a conversation, and he said he wanted to ask me a question, something that had been on his mind for a very long time. He wanted to know why, during the divorce, I didn't fight harder for him to come live with me. Can you imagine how difficult that conversation was? I had listened to the lawyer and the family therapist, who advised me to let him go. If there were issues with his dad, he needed to learn them on his own. He would have been resentful if those things had been brought to light at the time of the divorce. I had learned that, in order to protect my kids and keep them mentally sound, it just wasn't a good idea to badmouth my ex-spouse. Can that be difficult? Of course! It just wasn't in their best interests to involve them in our squabbles. I learned there were more productive ways to have difficult conversations. It took a lot of those conversations and a boatload of tears to get to a place of feeling healed.

CHAPTER

3

About a year after my ex-husband and I split up, I started seeing Rick. After everything the kids and I had been through, a relationship was the furthest thing from my mind. Life has a way of doing what it wants, right?

Rick is the father of Cari's first boyfriend. I got to know his first wife while the kids were dating. She was dealing with cancer treatments, and I ended up helping with some of her care until she passed away. My dealings with Rick had been mainly about his wife's care, and I did not get to know him very well during that time. I will admit, however, the first time I met him, I was struck by how handsome he was. At that time, I was dealing with a failing marriage, and he was trying to cope with a terminally ill wife, and I never gave it another thought.

Sometime later, when our kids were no longer an item, he called. It was weird at first, but we soon started talking every day. After a few weeks of phone conversations, he took me to dinner at a local hamburger joint and Best Buy, of all places. What a first date, right? Even so, from practically the first moment we spoke, we have just clicked. Rick is a man who is not at all interested in trying to be someone he's not. You know exactly what you get with him. He is sweet and goofy and has the best sense of humor. I was so attracted to that. It took some time for me to get it through my thick skull, but he is the real deal. He loves me for who I am and gives me the freedom to finally be myself. I have made lots of mistakes along the way, I have terrible pillow hair and dried drool in the morning, I am completely obsessed with dogs, I can be stubborn at times, I can cry at the drop of a hat, I have this weird love of all things Camaro, I am fiercely loyal, have had trust issues in the past—well you get the picture. Those were the things he got, and he loves me anyway! We have been together since that first date. Sometimes I wonder how we made it through those early years. We both brought our fair share of baggage to the relationship, and it can be challenging at times. Looking back, I think getting through those things helped solidify our relationship so that we would be able to survive what was on the horizon. Two years later, we were married. It was an adjustment for our kids, I think more so for mine. I don't think any of them were quite ready for it, and it was difficult for them, but they all eventually came around.

The year that Davey was graduating from high school, Rick had to sell his home. There were family-related issues involving inheritances etc. We had decided before this had come about that, once Davey graduated, we were going to leave California. The traffic and stress of living there were starting to take a toll on Rick. He was a truck driver, and if you have ever driven the San Diego Freeway, you are aware that it's nothing more than a gigantic parking lot. Cari had already transferred to UNLV (University of Nevada at Las Vegas), and we thought the timing was right. My goal was to convince Davey to come with us.

The house ended up selling right away, and it was still eight months until Davey graduated. With all the things going on, it was decided that we would move to Arizona and I would drive back every weekend so that I could still be a part of his life. I had a terrible time with this. I felt like I was abandoning him, but I did manage to go back every single weekend until his graduation. I got to take pics for his prom, go to his banquets and senior activities, and go to all his football games. Even if there was nothing going on, I went, even if he didn't necessarily want me there. Going out with friends or hanging with Mom? Sad to say, Mom wasn't always his first choice. But somehow we made it work. I had been fortunate when we moved to keep my medical-billing job. I now did it from home and was able to adjust my work schedule so that I could travel back and forth.

With everything that has happened since then, I still get upset thinking about the times I could have had with him had I stayed. I spent a lot of time trying to convince him to move to Arizona with me. He actually considered it, but in the end, Southern California was his home, and he loved it there and just could not bring himself to leave. This is one of my big regrets in life. I did what I felt like I had to do at that time, but I look at everything differently now. It's one of the things I wish I could get a do over with.

CHAPTER 4

After high school, Davey floundered a bit, uncertain of the direction he should take in life. As I have mentioned previously, the classroom was never a comfortable place for him. He got decent grades in school, but he only did what he had to do, and that was it. He attempted community college at our urging, but his heart just wasn't in it. Was I disappointed? Oh yeah, and I worried he wasn't going to find his way in the world. Every parent wants his or her child to succeed and be happy in life. I finally made peace with the fact that he just wasn't interested in college. He was a smart kid who had an insatiable thirst for knowledge. He would get where he needed to be in his own time and in his own way.

He also gained a significant amount of weight during this time. He was still eating like he did when he played football, only he was no longer burning those calories. He was miserable mentally and physically. He tried numerous diets and had committed to the gym. He would do well for a while, and then the weight would come right back on.

During this time, he started his first job for an airline at John Wayne Airport. He was the guy who loaded your luggage on the plane, and he also cleaned planes between flights. Did he love this job? Definitely not, but it paid the bills. After about six months, he got a job doing security for a defense department facility that stored fuel for the military. He stayed in that position for a few years. During that time, one of his supervisors had taken an interest in him, and he was eventually promoted to fuel operator. That's where his love of all things fuel-related began. He loved that job!

While he was busy with his job, his weight continued to suffer. His "come to Jesus" moment came when he went to the doctor for an unrelated issue. He was given some disturbing information. His blood pressure was high, his blood sugar was on its way to becoming diabetes, and he was having some sleep-apnea issues. The doctor was very blunt and told him that, if he did not do something and do it soon, he wouldn't live to see thirty. It was absolutely terrifying for all of us. I spent a lot of time beating myself up about how he had gotten to this place, where it had gone so wrong. He was only twenty-one years old! I decided to pull my head out of my rear and help him come up with a solution. We started doing extensive research about his options. He decided that maybe lap-band surgery was the answer. We made an appointment with the surgeon. After discussing all options, along with the risks, it was decided he would have gastric-bypass surgery.

It's a complicated process to even get the surgery scheduled. There were meetings with a team of experts, including a nutritionist and a psychologist. The psychologist was the one who opened his eyes to the fact that, in order to be successful with weight loss, he would have to deal with the emotional issues that got him there in the first place. Even so, a while after surgery, he remarked to me that, during that meeting, he really didn't pay a whole lot of attention to what she was saying. Ironically, that was the thing to which he should have paid the most attention. As so often happens, the emotional issues were the most complicated and difficult of all.

Several months after Davey started his weight-loss journey, he started a blog. He would write often about his weight struggles. He saw an interesting quote that he thought summed it up perfectly, "Every weight-loss program, no matter how positively it's packaged, whispers to you that you aren't right, that you aren't good enough. You're unacceptable, and you need to be fixed." He wrote how awful he felt when he was heavy. How unhealthy he felt and how his self-esteem was in the toilet. How he felt powerless at times to make the changes he needed to make. How, no matter where he was or whom he was with, someone would invariably comment about what a big guy he was. Or when he was playing football, someone would always make a comment about how lucky the team was to have a guy his size. He did not take these things as compliments. They burned him down to his soul. He became angry and started smoking cigarettes, something that terrified me. In his blog, he wrote that it wasn't until a few years later when he realized people weren't making fun of him; they were only stating their observations.

He had the surgery in May 2010. After he got home and he was on the road to wellness, he began to really feel confused about who he was. In his blog, he wrote, "I sounded the same, my hands and feet were the same, but when I looked in the mirror, I saw a stranger."

He was losing the weight quickly. Suddenly, clothes that had been bursting at the seams were now too big. His body was going through big changes, and they were happening fast. He would buy a new pair of pants, and two weeks later, they would be too big. He ended up losing over 150 pounds.

One of the more complicated issues for him? He had to learn about food all over. He had to learn what he could eat and what his new tummy could tolerate. A lot of that was experimentation. If one who has had gastric bypass consumes too much sugar in one sitting, then there is apt to be an episode of "dumping syndrome." Without going into too much detail, it involves stomach pain, vomiting, diarrhea, and a lot of sweating. It's not much fun, especially if you are out with the guys or on a date. He also had to learn that he could survive on small amounts of food. It sounds simple, but he had been consuming a lot of food for a long time. He would eat four ounces of something and feel full. His tummy would be full, but his head would mess with him and say, "We just started this meal, dude. You can't possibly be full." It took a while and was a lot of work, but he was finally able to change his mind-set about food. Food had always been a source of comfort for him, and that relationship no longer existed. In many societies, including ours, food is a social activity, and it was no different for Davey. He realized early on that just about everything he did socially revolved around food. He and his friends would eat every single time they hung out together. Every time he went anywhere, someone wanted to eat, something he had never paid attention to before.

His biggest struggles were by far the emotional ones. The psychologist that he had seen before his surgery had been right all along. He had learned that, if he wanted to keep the weight off, then he had to deal with the things that had gotten him there in the first place.

He could no longer just say he liked to eat; he had to figure out what was eating him.

During his weight-loss journey, as I have mentioned earlier, he was so confused about who he was now. It was a difficult time, his body going through all the changes and his emotions all over the place. He was thrilled at the weight loss, and he was now becoming more comfortable in his clothes and more aware of how he was changing. He was also terrified. He no longer had that wall of weight to hide behind. He was now going to have to put himself out there. For someone who had been hiding in plain sight a long time, that was a big step for him.

People were starting to notice his weight loss when he'd go out. Instead of hearing what a big guy he was, he was now hearing people tell him how amazing he looked. Other people, whom he had known for years, no longer recognized him. Women, some of whom had never given him the time of day, were now giving him appreciative looks. At first, he enjoyed the attention, but after a while, it started getting to him. He was still the same guy, after all; he just looked different. He would tell me that he would politely thank people for their kind comments, but privately, he began to wonder why they were all making such a big fuss. He wondered if people were really that shallow. When he was overweight, he always felt like he wasn't quite good enough. When people who never gave him the time of day were now all over him, well, it just added to his confusion. And to complicate matters even more, there were people in his life who would have preferred he not lose the weight. They were more comfortable with him being heavy. He used to wonder, why on earth people who cared about him would want him to look as he did when he was so miserable? He had a tough time with that one.

As you can see, significant weight loss is a journey. It is a journey for your body, of course, but mainly it's a journey of your mind and soul. Davey used to become furious when someone would casually mention that he had taken the easy way out. There is nothing easy about confronting your demons.

CHAPTER

5

After Davey had lost the weight and was well on his way to finding himself, he had a professional setback. He had been in his position of fuel operator for quite a while when he found out that his employer lost the bid for the new contract. The company that was taking over the contract did not need the same number of operators, and since he was one of the last hired operators, he was laid off. The employees had been told that, when the new company came in, they would all be hired back. They even had everyone fill out applications and go through interviews. He had no indication that he would not be rehired. Some of his coworkers started receiving their offers, but he and some of the newer guys never received one. He wasn't even notified he was laid off; he just never got an offer.

He was shocked and scared. He had loved that job and had hoped to make a career out of it. He applied for unemployment. In his blog, he wrote that filing for unemployment was one of the hardest things he had ever done. He had come so far, and he hated that feeling of needing assistance. He also knew in his heart that it wouldn't be for long. He needed a job, and he would get one. He knew he wanted to continue in the fuel business, but he put in applications anywhere and everywhere just to get something. It was a scary time as the economy was in "the worst recession since the great Depression." But Davey was not to be deterred. After a few weeks, he landed a position with a small refinery. It was a big pay cut from his previous position, but he knew he could learn a lot there, and well, it was a job, so he took it.

He had also always been interested in law enforcement, and during this time, he started the process of applying at police departments that were hiring. He applied to many departments. He would always do well on the written exams and physical-agility tests. He went through several interviews as well. For whatever reason, the job offers didn't come. He was finally accepted into one department, but because of the suffering economy, they implemented a hiring freeze. He finally realized that maybe it wasn't to be.

He worked in the refinery about a year and gained an invaluable amount of knowledge. Shortly thereafter, he heard one of the biggest refineries in the area was hiring, and he set his sights on getting that job. When he went in for the interview, he was told that 1,800 people had applied for 20 jobs. They had whittled the applicants to 400, and those were the people they would be interviewing. They spent about a month interviewing those candidates. Since he was among the first to be interviewed, it seemed like forever before he heard back. He got the news just before Christmas 2013. He got a job! Best news ever, right?

It was such a proud moment for him and for us. He had worked hard, and he had achieved his goal. It was a good company, and he was going to have such a future there. The day he finished his training, the day he was assigned to his new unit, was the day he died.

CHAPTER

6

One of Davey's quotes from his blog is "I've lost weight and I've gained life." Looking back, that statement really defines his journey. It's that quote that compelled me to write this book. See, to understand my journey of grief and healing, you need to know Davey and understand his journey.

The title of his first blog was "Falling Down to Find Your Way Back Up." In it, he talked a lot about how he felt before and after the surgery. The confusion about food. How could something that gave you such comfort make you hate the way you look? How he felt when someone would react negatively when they found out he took the supposedly "easy route" and had surgery. Not only would it make him angry; it would mess with his head big-time. He wondered why he was being judged, especially by people who had no idea what he had been going through. This was when he truly began his journey of discovering who he was and what his life meant. He wrote, "Everybody is on a journey. We have no idea about the battles they are fighting. And that just maybe we should learn not to judge one another." He became a fierce advocate for helping people learn not to judge others. He remained wholly committed to that for the rest of his life.

One of the reasons he started his blog was to put himself out there. That's quite a statement from someone who had spent the majority of his life hiding behind his weight. It really shows how much he grew emotionally in the last years of his life. He didn't just wake up one day emotionally healed. It was an ongoing process.

He started the blog because of the possibility that he could reach out to someone who was also struggling. There were so many times when Davey felt alone, that nobody really understood what he was going through, what he was feeling. Now, he had finally reached the point where he had become comfortable with who he was and wasn't too concerned with any negative reactions he may receive about his blog.

He wanted very much to be helpful without writing words that could hurt someone. He wrote, "Words can uplift and help or they can completely shatter you." He also needed to be honest. He told me that, if he couldn't be completely honest, then there was no point. He needed to share his truths. This is something I keep in mind while writing this. Some of my story is very difficult to relive. It's not easy to share your most private feelings. Davey felt strongly that, if you couldn't tell the whole story, then it wasn't worth telling at all. So I am following his lead.

Earlier in the story, I told you that, as a child, Davey had questions about everything and that never changed his whole life. I think it was an essential part of his growth. When he lost his job, he was in turmoil. He had a job he loved; he thought he had a future with a company he loved working for. He was unprepared for what happened. A conversation with his grandma opened his eyes. He mentioned to her that he just wasn't sure what direction he wanted to go in, and he asked for her opinion. She asked him only one question. She asked him what he wanted to do with his life. When you are feeling clueless about what you want, the question can be daunting. He had loved his job as a fuel operator and knew that he wanted to make a career of it. His childhood dream, though, had been to drive a sprint car, which is an open-wheel race car. He also knew in his heart that what he really wanted was stability, a future, a family. He would have loved to race, but he knew that, realistically, it's a tough way to make a living. He tucked that dream away for later.

Davey had begun to learn so much about himself. He used to say that learning things and then understanding what you have learned are two different things. Learning is about seeing things only for the results they provide. Understanding, however, necessitates examining the context of a decision and the basis of the process in the first place.

Where did that leave him? Trying to understand what he had learned had helped him to understand who he was. We used to say early on that Davey was an old soul. He finally figured that out for himself and, in doing so, wrote, "I found myself after figuring out that I had already done that. I have already messed up, have already learned and already understood." It was a moment for him.

He then wrote,

> This is how I became myself. Mistakes, embarrassment, harassment, addiction (cigarettes), pride, hate, love, death of people that I loved. Loss of pets that left my stomach in knots, horrible relationships, good relationships, rejections, strong morals, feeling like I did everything right when in fact I was doing everything wrong, losing my mind, finding it again, determination, strength, weakness, helping people, betrayals, but much greater loyalty. Conversations about life with family and friends, stepping out on a limb, breaking said limb, being stupid while being intoxicated, being a doormat, allowing myself to be used and using people.

And what he learned from all this? It's learning that you have to make mistakes to figure out who you *aren't*. He said that you have to take the action and the insight follows. That you just can't think your way into becoming yourself. He wrote that the mistakes he made were the most justified part of his life.

What came from his insight and hard work? Davey made me proud every day. He was unhappy and unhealthy, and he did the work. He was not an overnight success. It took a long time, and he was still on his journey of self-discovery at the time of his death. I think learning about yourself and growing emotionally are something that we should all continually work on, no matter how old we get. We are all works in progress!

Hard work had turned him into a confident young man. A man who would not change who he was for anyone else. A man who believed in strong morals and using good judgment. He understood that the hard work would continue and that he would not falter in his quest to learn and better himself. He would not falter in his quest to help others, to be strong for those who needed him.

In the last few years of his life, Davey had begun to study spirituality. We had never been a particularly religious family, but it was something in which he became really interested. As with everything, he learned as much as he could about different religions. He was very aware that we are all guided by a higher power. We used to have conversations about God and what it all meant. His journey and his death are how my spiritual journey have begun. It's something that brings me comfort now.

One of my very favorite things about him after he came into his own was his oh-so-wicked sense of humor. It just came alive. He had always been funny, but he had become downright hilarious. He was so quick with a comeback or joke. It's one of the things I miss so much.

One of the things that helped Davey grow was the friendships he had. One of his favorite quotes on the subject was "Your friends can either be an elevator or a cage." He had one group of guys with whom he was particularly close. They were always there for him, whether it be their advice, their families opening their homes to him at any time, and they were always honest with him. They would call him out on his BS as well. He was completely safe with them and really learned the true meaning of friendship. I will always be grateful that they were there for Davey through thick and thin. They had a bond that I'm sure continues to this day.

He also had a large group of friends with whom he stayed in contact throughout his life. After his accident, I will never forget how many people reached out to me. They all had the same message. They were going to miss his everyday texts, just to say what's up and to make sure they were okay. When these friends were dealing with issues, he would always do whatever he could to help. I have continued to hear from some of these people, and they tell me how much they miss his presence in their lives. Even if he only stopped by with a Starbucks, which, by the way, was Davey's very favorite. Once he discovered a drink there he could have after his surgery, it was an everyday thing for him. The baristas at Starbucks were among his favorite people.

After I had moved to Arizona, my mom and dad set up a regular Wednesday-night dinner with Davey. It was their way of making sure he was doing okay with my being gone. After my mom heard all these stories, she remarked that maybe she had had it backward. That those dinners were so that Davey could make sure they were okay.

As his mom, I have always thought that he was pretty darned special. I know what you must be thinking—every mother thinks her kids are special, but there were so many others who felt the same way. It has been soothing to my soul to hear their stories.

Over the years, he also had a group of older adults with whom he remained in contact. They included dads of some of his football buddies, people he met through his jobs and racing. He would always tell me they knew so much more than his friends did. I'll never forget that one of these men spoke at Davey's service. He was a Long Beach police detective and the father of one of his closest friends. While I don't remember his exact words, he considered Davey to be another one of his sons, and it brought some peace to my heart.

Davey also loved kids. A good friend of his had a daughter with severe autism. She has had many struggles, and Davey just loved her. He was able to sometimes reach her when others could not. He and his dad became involved in a charity for kids with autism. They spent a lot of time working with this charity and the kids. He used to tell me those kids were another reason he felt strongly about not judging others. He would become furious when someone would judge a child, especially because they were children! And people generally had no idea what was going on with these kids, yet they could be nasty and judgmental.

Watching my son's transformation from a confused and unhappy young man to someone who was kind, confident, and engaging was a sight to behold. At the time of his death, he was as happy as I had ever seen him. It is one of the things that are so damn hard for me. My son had had some major struggles in his life. He recognized he was unhappy and worked so hard to turn his life around. Nobody did it for him; he did it himself. Was it easy? As you have read, it was definitely not easy, but he persevered. We loved and supported him every step of the way, but it was all him. He was, and continues to be, such an inspiration to us and to the people whose lives he touched. He did all this by the age of twenty-five! Some of us, including me, spend a lifetime trying to figure it all out. For him to go through all that and then we lose him? It made things worse for me for a while. More about that later.

CHAPTER

7

On April 27, 2014, we got the call just before midnight. Cari called and said that Davey had been in a car accident. She did not have any other information. I was in Arizona, and she was in Las Vegas. We both sat by the phone and waited for my ex-husband to get to the hospital so we could find out what the heck had happened. When he arrived, he was told that Davey was already gone. He had died instantly upon impact. Please bear with me here; it's awful reliving this. When I first got the call that he had been in an accident, it never occurred to me that it was going to be so terrible. I remember thinking that I hoped it wouldn't affect his new job. When Cari called to tell me he had passed away, I remember screaming that she was lying to me. I was hysterical. The next several hours were a blur to me. I vaguely remember my mom coming over and sitting with me while I screamed. I also remember thinking that I should have known my baby was in trouble. A mother's intuition, right? I had nothing. That is something that I have never come to terms with, and I'm not sure why. Would it have been any easier if I had known that something bad was going to happen? I think not.

When morning arrived, we left to go to California. I was in such a hurry to get there. I kept thinking that, if I hurried and got there, I would see him and this whole nightmare would go away. It's about a six-hour drive from Prescott to Lakewood, and that drive took forever. We were in our truck. Rick and my mom were in the front, and I was lying in the back seat with my eyes closed. All of a sudden, I saw Davey. I had a vision of him sitting on his motorcycle, completely dressed in his leathers and helmet. He was surrounded by the most beautiful blue sky. I didn't realize it at that time, but I think he was letting me know he was okay, about to ride off into his next adventure When we pulled up to the house, I could see his work boots sitting on the front porch. Do you know that's one of the things that haunt me to this day? Why this particular sight should be so riveting is a mystery to me.

We went inside, and there were so many people there. Some of them I knew; most of them I did not. I was in such a fog that I don't remember a whole lot. When I saw Davey's father, the tears flowed again. Whatever had happened between us seemed completely unimportant at that moment. We were just two grieving parents trying to understand the nightmare that had unfolded. I do remember a few things. I couldn't bring myself to go into Davey's room. I also remember a gentleman there who was being loud and was laughing a lot. I recall wondering how he could be acting so inappropriately. Now though, I think maybe he was uncomfortable with the shock and sadness in the room and wasn't sure how to act. In the room, there was also someone sharing details about the accident. It was as if he were performing. Why? I just couldn't listen to that person. He also showed me Davey's watch that he had been wearing at the time of the accident. All that was left was the watch itself. The band had come off at the time of impact. I was shaken to my very soul by all this. Back then, I had a really hard time understanding why this person felt the need to share this stuff. Over time, I have come to understand he was in shock too, and it's best not to judge his actions. At that time, though, I wanted to punch him in the face.

Davey had gone with his buddies to watch some street races. As was customary, if someone had had too much to drink, Davey was the designated driver. He did not drink much at all, so it was always up to Davey to get his not-so-sober friends home. After he had dropped his friend off at home, for unknown reasons, he had pulled over to the side of the road. Because using a handheld device in California is illegal, the police speculated that he had pulled over to use his phone. He was not, however, on his phone at the time of the accident. As he started out, he was going to make a U-turn to return to his friends. At that moment, two cars that were street-racing with their headlights off came barreling down the street. As Davey started his turn, he was hit by one of the cars in the driver's door. The business across the street had a camera attached to the building, and the accident was recorded on the camera.

After the accident, the cowards took off. They made no attempt to see if Davey was hurt, nor did they even call 911. Apparently, they just couldn't be bothered. That is something I will never forget or understand. They left my baby there to die alone.

By the time we had arrived in California, they had been arrested and were in jail. I didn't spend too much time thinking about them back then. I was trying to hold on to my sanity and take care of my baby and Cari, who turned out to be the strongest of any of us.

I did not want to hear all the details of the accident, and what I have told you is all I know. I did not want to know the extent of Davey's injuries. I wanted to remember him whole and beautiful. I have not seen the video. I will never look at it. I have not seen Davey's car, and I have no idea what happened to it. In a weird way, I used to think about the car. As I told you before, we are a family of car lovers, and I knew how much he loved that car. He would have been so upset knowing she was sitting in a junkyard. I did hear she was damaged beyond repair and has probably been demolished.

My ex-husband and I are completely different in how we have dealt with this tragedy. He needed to know every detail. He kept rehashing them over and over. He wanted justice, and he wanted it now. He wanted the men responsible to go to prison and never come out. I wanted those things too. I was just not as vocal as he was.

The next few days were and will always remain a blur to me. There are a few things I remember clearly, however. That first night after arriving in California, we checked into a hotel. By the time we got there, we were all exhausted and emotionally spent. There was a kitchenette in the room, and I sat down at the small kitchen table that was against a wall. Right over my head was a light fixture. All of a sudden, that light flashed on and off three times. None of the other lights in the room did anything. At that time, I had limited knowledge of afterlife communications. I realized later that it must have been another message from Davey. He was trying hard to let me know he was okay. Thinking back, it seems strange to me that I even remember that incident, as I was barely functioning.

The next day, I was hit with the reality that I needed to plan a funeral for my baby boy. No parent should ever have to do this. There were so many details to be handled. In my state, it was completely overwhelming to me. I honestly don't know how I made it through any of it. I was grateful to have Rick by my side. He was my rock and my voice when I couldn't form a coherent thought, let alone say it.

I do remember the lady at the funeral home asking me if I was okay, that I looked a "little dazed." I actually wanted to scream at her. I had just lost my baby. How in the world did she think I should look? Dressed nicely and well put together? Again, I get that people don't always know how to act in these terrible situations. But sheesh, she plans funerals, for cripe's sakes; she has probably seen hundreds of "dazed" faces.

Another difficult decision was trying to decide about burial versus cremation. I just kept thinking that this could not be real. He was only twenty-five. We decided that cremation was the way to go. I wanted my son's ashes with me. I have made it clear that, when I die, my son's ashes will be spread with mine.

The next day, we all went into Davey's room and started cleaning out his clothes. Why did we do this? I have no idea. That stands out to me as one of the stranger things we did that week. I think we just had no idea what to do about anything. We were in such shock and in this total fog. We were taking the items that we wanted and donating the rest. There were also bills and papers to go through, but that was set aside for another day.

While in California, we were asked to go to the hospital to see Davey. At first, I was adamant that I didn't want to see him. I had no desire to see him with all the injuries. I didn't want to remember him that way. In the end, I decided to go. Otherwise, I feared I could never believe he was gone.

When we got there, they took us to the morgue in the basement of the hospital. For some reason, it being in the basement really bothered me. The lady who escorted us down there explained that there was still medical equipment attached to him. It could not be removed until the autopsy was done. He was also an organ donor, and some of his organs had been removed. They had him covered up to his neck with a sheet.

This is, by far, the most difficult thing I have ever done. My baby was lying there with a tube in his nose. He looked so beautiful, so peaceful. Other than a small cut on his forehead, he did not look injured in any way. But I continue to be haunted by that day. I regret that I was so hysterical that I didn't kiss my baby goodbye. I didn't want to feel him and feel that his body was cold. I wanted warmth and him alive. I wish I had had the courage to hold him and kiss him. His father had that courage. He went right over and kissed his forehead.

He died on Saturday night, and the funeral was planned for the following Friday. My beautiful daughter and her friend Jenny planned the service. I was useless and just could not help them. She wrote and delivered the eulogy herself. She and Davey had been so close; it was only fitting that she be the one to stand up there and honor her brother.

My ex-husband wanted a big celebration of life after the service. He had a friend who owned a restaurant at the pier in San Pedro. It had a large banquet room, and he insisted it be held there. I didn't think Davey would have liked something so elaborate. Davey was a total barbecue-in-the-backyard type of guy, and that's what I would have preferred. I fought with his dad about it for a while, but he would not be deterred, and I just didn't have the energy to continue the fight.

I had to buy something to wear to my son's funeral. We wanted everyone to dress casually because Davey was just that kind of guy. We also went and got our nails done. For a funeral. Who on earth would have cared if my nails had been chipped? I was on autopilot. My mind was just following my body around, being noncontributory.

The service was held at the mortuary chapel in Palos Verdes, California, on Friday, May 2, 2014. It was a beautiful spring day. Palos Verdes is a beautiful city near the ocean. It really fits the model for what California living is all about. Since Davey was a true Californian through and through, it really was a fitting place to have the service.

I don't remember a lot of details about the service, but I do remember how the love for Davey was shining like a beautiful big sunrise in that room. It was packed inside, and people had to stand outside. My baby girl pulled herself together and gave the most lovely, heartfelt eulogy about her brother. Several people then stood up and spoke about our Davey. After it was over, Cari, her dad, and I released doves into the air. I don't remember much more, other than the fact that I sobbed throughout. I also remember Rick holding me up so I wouldn't fall.

After the service, we all went to the celebration of life. They had done some really nice things. There were pictures of him on all the tables, and there was a large video screen showing pictures of Davey throughout his life. There were so many people there, but again, it's mostly a blur to me. We stayed for a while, but my heart really wasn't in it. One thing that stood out glaringly to me was the fact that my son had just died, yet everyone was eating and drinking as if it were a party or some festive occasion. People were not actually partying by any means, but I just couldn't come to grips with the whole "celebration of life" thing. It just wasn't where I wanted to be. I wanted to be with my son.

The next morning, we headed home to Arizona.

CHAPTER 8

As I have said previously, the two men (I have a really difficult time referring to them as men, but the names that I think they deserve are probably not appropriate to print) who did this were arrested and put in jail the morning after the accident. The passenger in the car that hit Davey was bailed out, but the driver stayed in jail throughout. We were assigned a wonderful deputy district attorney who was there every step of the way with us. We had no experience with this type of thing, and he walked us through the process each and every time we were there. I had never been in a courtroom before, and needless to say, it wasn't like what you saw on TV. When I walked in the first time, it wasn't at all what I expected. It was dark and dreary. There was brown everywhere. And it smelled terrible. Just what you imagine misery would smell like. There were people inside, and they were all doing their jobs, but I remember thinking that they all looked disconnected. I guess working with the situations that they have to deal with every day requires a certain amount of detachment.

There were several hearings and delays. Rick and I would take off work each and every time and drive to the Compton, California, courthouse. Davey's father and Cari were also there every time. At one point, Davey's dad lost it and went after one of the men. Of course, the court did not act favorably toward my ex, and he was appropriately scolded. Privately though, I wouldn't have minded if my ex had throttled the guy. Many of the delays were because of the shenanigans of the defense attorney for the passenger of the car. I understand he was hired to do a job. His job was to keep his thug, er, client, out of jail. I get it. Nevertheless, his behavior was abhorrent. He spent most of his time claiming his client was a victim in all this. He even insinuated that he felt threatened by my brother and me. We happened to see him in the parking lot after court one day and we "looked at him funny." When your entire life has been upended and you are basically going through the motions, it made his claim seem even more ridiculous. At that time, I didn't have the enough energy to hurt a fly. Looking back now, however, I would not be opposed to punching him in the nose if I ever had the chance. Not really, but I sure enjoyed writing it.

Each and every time we went to court, the families of the defendants were there. Apparently, neither of them had ever been in trouble before, and their families were struggling too. Did I reach out to those families? I did not. Do I regret that? That remains an unanswered question. I was angry at them back then, mainly because they hired that horrible attorney. I get it now though. They were doing what they needed to do, just like we were doing. Sometimes, I think Davey would have reached out to them and that maybe I should have done the same. But at that time, I wasn't thinking about it.

I want to be clear here. My anger at them was because they left the scene. People do stupid things. Street racing is incredibly dangerous. And my son and his friends used to go watch those races. But these guys were not racing where the races were going on. Should they have known better? Of course. Did they need to race over one hundred miles per hour with their headlights off? Of course not. They were stupid, and they were reckless. Having said that, I would have looked at them a whole lot differently had they stopped and tried to help. They had no way of knowing that Davey was already gone. And had my son had someone with him when he died, it would have made it a little more bearable for me.

After endless delays and hearings, we finally had a date for sentencing. The judge remarked that what happened was such a terrible tragedy for everyone involved. I thought that was an odd thing for him to say. Their families would move on from this. Ours? Not so much.

We were all invited to address the court before sentencing. At first, I wasn't going to. I have always been fairly shy and have lived a lot of my life on the sidelines. I was learning from counseling that I have a voice, and it was way past time for me to start using it. I wanted those two young men to know what they had done to our family. I wanted them to know what kind of man Davey was. I wanted them to look at me when I spoke. All that happened except the last thing. Neither of those cowards had the courage to look at me when I spoke to them. I wasn't terribly surprised. They had already shown the world what kind of cowards they were when they left the scene. I do have the satisfaction of knowing they heard me loud and clear.

The driver was sentenced to two years in prison for killing my son. The passenger was given something called felony probation and did not have to serve any time. The driver served one year and then was released. Apparently, California has an overcrowded prison system, and he was released early for good behavior.

Reading back over this, I realize I still sound a little bitter. Maybe so, but I really don't think about those two anymore. In fact, I couldn't even tell you the name of the passenger. I simply don't care what happens to them or how they live their lives. I have read about families of victims forgiving the people who have killed their family members. I feel no reason to forgive them or not forgive them. I just don't care about them. When I spoke to them at sentencing, I asked them to try and live a life that honors Davey after this was all behind them. Have they attempted to do so? I have no idea; neither of them has ever tried to contact me.

CHAPTER 9

Before I get to the rest of my journey, I want to share with you the story of my daughter, Cari, and the extraordinary relationship that she and Davey shared.

I have forever told anyone who would listen to my chatter that I have never been able to believe how damn lucky I am that these two wonderful humans were given to me. These wonderful, kind, decent kids are mine! To this day, even after everything that I have endured, I still consider myself to be extraordinarily blessed that I was chosen to be their mom. Did we go through struggles and challenges? Sure, we did. Did I make a boatload of mistakes along the way? Absolutely. Yet they survived my mistakes and became just the best people ever!

Cari and Davey were four years apart in age. I had suffered a miscarriage in between the two of them. At first, I worried they would be too far apart in age to be close. I was 100 percent wrong. From day one, they connected in a way that brought pure joy to my heart. Did they fight and get on each other's nerves? On occasion.

Well, probably more often than that. One thing that was a staple in our home is they were taught that, at the end of the day, they needed to have each other's backs. They always did look out for each other.

They both grew up loving music. It spoke to them in a way that I never really understood. They both have such a hilarious sense of humor. The jokes and quick comebacks that flew between them kept us entertained regularly. They were there to comfort each other during the difficult times that we experienced as a family. They taught each other about kindness, loyalty, and honesty.

As they grew older, they were both very busy with school and sports. Even so, they managed to stay a big part of each other's lives. It was sometimes difficult to try to find time to have dinner together, but we made it work.

When Cari moved to Nevada to go to college, it was hard on all of us, but I think for Davey it was a little tougher. Cari was always the buffer when there were family issues. They looked out for each other, and I think he felt a little alone when she left. I know too that, at times, he was a little resentful that he was left to deal with said family issues all on his own. I tried to be as supportive as I could, but it wasn't the same, and I knew he needed his sister at times.

They communicated often, even if it was only to throw out a friendly insult or joke. Thank goodness for texting. It was easy for us all to stay connected. Getting a quick text from either kid letting me know all was well kept Mama a happy camper.

Cari would try to go home often, and they started a tradition that continued up to the very end. She would wait up for him at night to get home from work, and they would put in a movie to watch. Without fail, Cari would be asleep in five minutes. I can just see Davey shaking his head at her with a little poke in the arm. "Wake up, dork."

The best part of their relationship? They could talk to each other about anything. I loved that they had that. Everyone needs someone to whom they can confide anything.

After she graduated from college, Cari spent the next few years working in different parts of the country for a luxury hotel brand, even going as far as Atlanta. Those years were a little difficult for all of us as we just didn't get to see her as often. It was good for her; she got to experience different ways of life, and she met some incredible people along the way.

After a few years, she settled back in Las Vegas and took a job as the director of sales for a corporate team-building, start-up company. She has found her niche there. She also met her fiancé, John, and they are busy planning their wedding.

Davey drove back to Vegas with her when she moved. From then on, we all got to see one another often. We spent as much time together as our schedules would allow. One of my favorite memories during these years is Christmas 2013. We celebrated a few days early as Davey had to get back to start his new job. It was the most wonderful Christmas we have ever had together.

We were here in Arizona with Rick and my parents. It was full of love and laughter and just lots of fun. I remember thinking at that time, "So this is what a Hallmark Christmas is." Davey's accident was just four months later. I have spent a lot of time reflecting about that holiday. It was so perfect and I wonder if it was because we were about to lose him.

As I mentioned earlier, after the accident, Cari took it upon herself to plan Davey's service. She was in shock and just as devastated as the rest of us, but she showed a toughness that I've never seen before. She decided on her own that she would do his eulogy and lead the service. Even in my shock, I was adamant that it be someone who knew Davey. There was no way I was going to let the people who run the funeral home speak about my son when they never knew him.

She stood up on that podium, and with a strong voice that was full of love, she honored her brother in a way that nobody else could have. I would like to share her words; they reflect the bond they still have.

Hey, baby, what's up?

As most of you know, Davey always opened a conversation with that line. I'm going to try my hardest to get through this, I want to get it right.

I knew there was going to be a lot of people here, but wow! I am just in awe. As I have been most of my adult life of Davey. Don't you ever wonder how one guy could be so insightful? Or, how the advice he gave was way beyond his years? Davey understood things that neither I nor his parents even understand now. As I read through his blogs, I was just amazed at the insight they provided. Not only into his life, but into my own as well. I think the only way to truly honor Davey's memory is to proceed with his service using most of his words.

One of the quotes that has stuck with Davey over the years is a single one. Passion is about finding the one thing that makes you smile in the morning. Davey had so many passions, we can tell by the diverse group of people joined here today. One of his greatest passions in life was cars. Davey stated that "cars have shown me wonderful things, taught me wonderful things, and most importantly, introduced me to the most beautiful people on the planet. Not beautiful because of looks, or because of what car they tend to obsess over, but beautiful because of heart, because of passion." One of Davey's driving forces was encouraging people to find those passions. He said that many people live their lives waking up every day with nothing to smile about. He encouraged us to find our true passions. He shared that with us, not to inform us on one of his passions, or how it came about, but to show us that in life when something jumps up and bites you in the ass, remember why it did. Remember the people who were a part of it. Try to remember how you feel. In this world, there is a reason behind everything. Take advantage of finding that reason. He then advised that when you do find that passion, cherish it and put it in front of everything. Because at the end of the day, you know that the juice is worth the squeeze. Davey then said, "[All right, all right], I know that last sentence is from the 2004 movie, *The Girl Next Door* but damn, did Emile Hirsch's character Matthew Kidman nail it!

In finding our passions, Davey, who was beyond his years, also encouraged all of us here to make mistakes. One of the most important things that Davey said he learned during his stint of life is you have to make mistakes to find out who you aren't. You take the action and the insight follows. You can't really think your way into becoming yourself. He stated that mistakes were the most justified part of his life. "You will never get the benefit of making mistakes, yes, I said benefit, if you don't make them. You must harness those mistakes for your own benefit. Mistakes can point you to something you don't know, deepen your knowledge, show you what matters and what doesn't, it can serve as a warning, point out hidden faults, show us that we are like others, bring out relationship problems, show you your authentic self, show you when you are not listening. You must expect mistakes as a normal part of growth and development."

Davey wants us all to be thankful for the past and what it has taught us, but to understand that it's just not the mistakes that we have made that truly define us.

[Okay], what have we learned from Davey so far? We must find our passions and it's ok to make mistakes during the process.

As Davey progressed through his blog, you can truly start to see a change within him. An even more insightful person developing. As all of us here know, Davey never judges others. He didn't see a reason. Another one of Davey's driving passions in life was to help people. He says, "instead of being selfish, why don't you take a step back and see what you can do for someone else. My greatest friendships have started and been kept by helping the people closest to me. Why? Because I care about them." A quote from his blog says "[T]he next time that you meet someone, just stop for a second. Look at how they are, appreciate their struggles whether you know what they are or not. People tend to forget what other people go through, our society has become more about me and what's wrong with me. People are absolutely beautiful in every form, as long as you take the time to find out. Be positive, fight for everything you have. Be the best individual you can be. Be different in every way possible. Next time you meet someone, don't give them a handshake, give them a hug. It takes courage to be different, not follow the norm."

Another of my most favorite quotes from Davey's blogs in regards to people is this, "try and find something to focus on when you are feeling down. Motivation can be anywhere, you just have to open up enough to find it. Be proud of who you are and strive to be better.

Appreciate people's stories, learn from them, be a part of them. Things will get hard and things may get in your way, but keep your head down and fight. Open your heart to the world and I guarantee it won't let you down. The true measure of a good man is how he can treat someone who can do him absolutely no good."

By learning these new lessons before most people do, Davey was able to accomplish so much in such a short time frame. He was able to amass a wonderful group of close friends, who are here now and who would do anything for my brother. I know, because I have personally seen it this past week. Davey earned a position with Tesoro—a position that eighteen hundred people applied for and only twenty received. He learned to build a beautiful car that he was so proud of. He followed his passion into motorcycle riding and finally drove the sprint car that he always dreamed of. So what does this tell us? It tells all of us here that we can accomplish anything. We have solid evidence in Davey that when we find our passions, make mistakes and help people, that we can truly accomplish anything.

In conclusion, Davey reminds us that "at the end of the day, to stand by your decisions, and above all else be proud of your accomplishment, no matter what negative responses you get. Follow your heart in every situation you encounter because it will always steer you in the right direction. If you are unhappy, change it, no matter how hard it may be. You can't make everyone happy, but you can make yourself happy. Stop texting people, phone calls are so much cooler. If you're bored, find something better. You don't have to settle. Do not take anything you don't deserve from anyone. Treat people with respect. Karma is real, doing good for people will pay off. Make educated decisions, not stupid mistakes. Things will work out the way they are supposed to, take each day as it comes, live in the moment. Don't forget to smile more, laugh more, sing more and love more. And most of all, follow your bliss."

It was very difficult for me to tell this part of the story. I want readers to really get a sense of Cari and Davey's relationship. But boy, reliving this part is painful, to say the least.

PART

2

Grieving and Healing

CHAPTER

10

First, I would like to reiterate that I am not a professional writer. I am, first and foremost, a mom. This is not a step-by-step survival manual of how to get through crushing grief. This is just my story and my opinions. Maybe other grieving parents can see themselves in my story and realize that, even though the pain will never go away entirely; with time, it becomes more bearable.

When we returned to Arizona following the funeral, I had no idea what I was supposed to do. Was I just supposed to tuck myself back into my life and continue on as if everything were normal? I was still in a complete state of shock. And quite frankly, I wasn't interested in continuing on without Davey. I wanted to be with my son. I was consumed with worry about him in heaven. As a mom, you always worry about where your kids are and if they are safe and happy. This was no different. I wanted to be with him, and I seriously considered suicide. I have always been curious about what could drive a person to suicide. I have read that, in a lot of cases, those people felt their loved ones would be better off without them; that's why they do it.

That is never the case. They leave train wrecks of families behind. My reasoning had nothing to do with my loved ones. I was only consumed with being with my baby and making sure he was okay.

I was despondent and completely out of control. I had decided that, when I got home, I would go back to work. I work for a urologist from home, doing billing and collections. Somewhere in my fog, I knew that at some point I would need to work. My boss depends on me to get the billing done. Without me doing my job, his bills don't get paid. So off to work I went. Was that the best decision at the time? Probably not, but when you're consumed by grief, it becomes difficult—no, impossible—to think clearly. I thought it would perhaps be a distraction from my pain. Wrong. There are no distractions, nor can there be. I barely functioned, yet I somehow managed to get some stuff done.

After being home for a week, we had to go back to California to pick up Davey's ashes. We had decided to split the ashes between Davey's dad and me. I later learned that some people have an objection to ashes being divided, for a variety of reasons. I, however, have no such objections. He was loved by both his parents, and that's just the way it was.

I brought ashes home on Mother's Day. Oh, the irony, right? Mother's Day will never be the same for me. I have my Cari, and I treasure every moment with her. But it just is never going to be the same. I completely avoid social media on that day. It's very hard to see pictures with all the smiling moms and their babies. Does that sound petulant? Perhaps, and I would never want to see another mom live through what I have survived. But I was cheated out of a lifetime with Davey and it's just the way I feel.

Before we made the drive back to California, I had decided that I wanted a tattoo that honored Davey. I have never ever contemplated a tattoo; it wasn't something that had ever interested me. In my crazy, fogged state of mind, it was one thing that became glaringly clear to me. Davey had a few tattoos, and he loved them. He had a friend, Kevin, who was a tattoo artist. He did all of Davey's tattoos. I remember when he got the first one. I was so against it. I was afraid people would judge him. Who the heck cares? Some of the things I used to worry about were so pointless. It took a tragedy for me to realize that many of the things we worry about in this life are actually trivial. Davey felt that those tattoos were the perfect way to express himself. You know what? They were beautiful and tasteful, and Davey loved them. They were such an expression of who he was. His favorite quote was "Follow your bliss." It was tattooed on his arm, where it could be seen by everyone. That statement meant everything to him. He was well on his way in his journey to finding that bliss.

I called Kevin and set up the appointment. I now have a beautiful "Follow your bliss" tattoo on the inside of my forearm with four interlocking hearts. I absolutely love it. Every day, I am reminded that I need to get to that place of bliss.

After returning home with his ashes, I had to figure out what to do with them. I was not about to put them in a closet, as was suggested by more than one person. I know people were trying to help me. Hiding them was not going to make what happened go away. I had purchased an urn that I thought fit Davey to a T. It had a motorcycle on top. His motorcycles were one of the joys in his life. There was nothing like a long ride to clear his head and revive his spirit. I found a beautiful spot under a window in my living room, and there it sits. He is always here with me, and it is a comfort for me to have him close by.

After I got settled back at home, I spent my days alternately crying, working, screaming, and wishing I were dead. That was my life for a while. I would talk to Davey's dad at times, but it was just too painful for either of us. Before the accident, our relationship could run hot and cold at times and had been that way for several years since the divorce. He needed to keep rehashing everything to do with the accident, and I didn't want to hear any of it. Then the issue of lawyers came up. We needed the help of a lawyer because of the legal issues that were being thrown at us from every direction. We had no idea how to navigate through any of it. I thought we should get a lawyer with whom we could work together. He was angry and wanted a lawyer who would do litigation against anyone and everyone connected to the accident. It was a way to channel his rage at what had happened. I get it. While I understood where he was coming from, it was not the way I wanted to handle things. We agreed to disagree and have not spoken since. I now realize the decision not to speak was partly based on the lawyer issue, but mainly it was just too painful for both of us.

After about a month, I had a doctor's appointment for something unrelated. He took one look at me and told me I needed a grief counselor and I needed it now. He also recommended a low dose of an antidepressant. I have read various opinions about whether one should take them when grieving, that perhaps they mask the pain and you don't properly heal from the grief. At that point, I just didn't see how anything was going to help me. He made me promise to make an appointment with the therapist and at least start the medication until I could get in to see her.

So I did, but I only did so because I had made a promise. I was certainly not very optimistic that I would ever feel better. The only thing that would make me feel better was Davey. Apparently, that was just not going to happen. Although if I am being completely honest, I was starting to have an inkling that I could not continue down this road forever and that just maybe I wasn't making my son in heaven proud of me.

I can tell you now that those two things saved my life. The medication did not mask the pain at all. Together with therapy, I survived. Three years in, and I can tell you that nothing will ever mask the pain. Ever. As time has gone on, however, I have learned to live with that pain. I have come to terms with the fact that it's never going away, although it's not nearly as fierce as it was for a very long time. I am still seeing the therapist for continued healing and guidance about how to navigate this life that I am now being forced to live. I remember telling her right off the bat that I did not want to be bitter and angry over what happened for the rest of my life. One thing that has been absolutely clear to me since the accident is that I want to honor my son's memory, and I couldn't do it by being ugly and bitter inside. She told me then and has repeated it many times that losing a child is probably one of the most difficult things a person can go through.

I spent a lot of time trying to figure out why this happened, to him and to his family. Why did my parents have to lose their only grandson? Why was someone in the prime of his life taken when he had just performed a good deed? I learned through therapy that there are no good answers to my questions and there never will be. It took me a long time to come to terms with that. I like answers. I have always lived my life with a black-and-white personality. Not having those answers and learning that there was a gray area in my life was a tough thing for me. Once I asked the therapist why Davey went through all those challenges, lose the weight, get his dream job, only to die in an accident. Do you know what she said? She told me it was pretty amazing that he had accomplished a lifetime of things in a short time on earth, that it was a blessing, and I was privileged to see my son do precisely that. Maybe I would feel worse had he died and not realized his potential. I admit that I was pissed off when she said it was a blessing. I do see it now, however. Sometimes I wonder if maybe Davey knew on some level that his life would be short and he crammed in as much as he possibly could.

I was slowly trying to get back into my old routine while realizing that everything was different and would never be the same. As anyone who knows me will tell you, I thrive on routine. I think it goes back to my first marriage, where everything was always so chaotic. Once I was away from that situation, I discovered that routine and less clutter were the ways for me to have some sense of control in my life. I was completely clueless about how to survive now. Everything I had known and believed was different. Imagine floating on a raft in the ocean, powerless against where the currents will carry you, not knowing if you would ever see land again, with no idea how to get yourself to shore and then being able to find your footing if you did make it to shore. That was me. For a long time.

Going through something so traumatic changes everything. And I mean everything. The old Debbie is gone, never to return. I had to learn to function in a world I didn't really want to be a part of. But I had my daughter, who needed me, and my husband, who had, and continues to have, my back throughout all this. There will also be a time when my parents may need my assistance as they get older. I want to be present for all of them. It's important to me to never let any of them down.

I have continued with therapy. I was going every week at first, but I'm now going about once a month. She helped me to understand how grief works, that, over time, the grief would start to ease up. She described grief as coming in big waves that engulf you. I had to learn to ride those waves. She was right. After a long while, those waves began to get a little smaller and a little less intense. I must admit though, I was being stubborn and hardheaded at times. I had convinced myself that, if I started to feel better, I wasn't honoring my son. Guess what? I was being ridiculous. Spending your days screaming like a lunatic does not honor your loved ones, for cripe's sake! Having said that, I firmly believe that your grief never really goes away. It does lessen over time, and I have learned to live with it, but it's always lurking in the back of my heart, ready to rear its ugly head when the occasion arises.

In the beginning, I thought of nothing else. I relived each and every horrible memory all day, every day. I was plagued with guilt. He was in a car accident. I'm not sure what I had to feel guilty about. The grieving mind does what it wants, and I was so depressed. Once moment I would tell myself that I need to pull it together and resume my life. The next moment, I would be lying in bed crying and not caring about anything. I would go out to do errands and, out of nowhere, start bawling again. I would be driving down the street and hear a song that reminded me in some way of Davey and start screaming. I at least had the good sense to pull over until I could calm down. I have this horrible memory of being in the grocery store and sobbing over a box of Kraft mac and cheese. It was one of Davey's favorites growing up. When I walked by the box in the grocery-store aisle, the tears started flowing as soon as I saw it. I had no control over those tears. The poor people in the grocery store were wondering what the heck was so heartbreaking about mac and cheese!

Those days were my life for a while. It was like I had one foot in the past part of my life and one foot planted firmly in my life right now. I was stuck and had no idea how to move forward. Not only was I depressed; I was damn mad! For some reason, I expected people to understand my pain. Why should they? It's not like I wore a shirt that said "Beware, grieving mom." Most of the time, however, I just lived in my fog. I didn't care much about anything.

One of the things I remember clearly is wondering why everything in the universe continued with life after what had happened. We had been knocked completely off our axis, yet the world just went right on. In my grief, it was one of the things I thought about often.

I remember the first time I laughed out loud a few months after the accident. I was totally shocked. That simple thing set me back a bit. How dare I laugh when my baby was gone! My very next thought was that I had somehow betrayed him. I went through this vicious cycle for a long time. I was caught up in my pain, and a part of me kept telling myself that I was betraying him if I got better. It sounds silly, I know. Nobody wants to be in this kind of pain. I was in this constant state of confusion, feeling one minute that I needed to get better so that I could properly honor his memory, and the next feeling, if I did get better, I was betraying him.

It took me a long time, but I eventually figured out that I was not living a life that honored Davey.

Something I wrestled with for a long time is that I must have done something to make me deserving of such a tragedy. Or did Davey do something so that it was decided his life be cut short?

Those things sound silly to me now. Of course we didn't do anything. I don't believe we were receiving some kind of karmic payback, but that's where my mind wandered at times. We are not always completely rational beings, after all.

CHAPTER 11

I have told you previously how Rick and I met and that we had some major challenges early on with dealing with our pasts and blending our families. We were put to the test again big time after the accident.

As you know, I wasn't coping well at all. One of the things I would do is scream at Rick, often for no apparent reason. Or I would scream at him because he didn't fold the socks properly (or some other unimportant task). I was out of control, and he would take the brunt of it. Anyone who knows my husband knows that he is a fixer. He has taken on that role his entire life. But there was no fixing me. When I was raging, he would do his best to comfort me, and when that didn't work, he would go out to his garage for a while. There were times I just wanted to be angry, and it would piss me off when he tried to make me feel better.

Rick has been there every step of the way through this journey. He has held me countless hours while I screamed and cried. He drove me back and forth to California many times without complaint. He hung pictures of Davey; he did whatever needed to be done to keep me on my feet. He did the majority of the household duties when I could not. He dealt with my depression and bad moods by trying to be whatever I needed him to be. And that man never uttered a word of complaint.

As time went on, however, he did become a little frustrated, I think. Not because of what I had lost, but because he more or less had become my verbal punching bag. When I think back to those first several months and the way I spoke to him sometimes, I am horrified. Could I have done things differently? Maybe, but I was in a bad place and didn't have a whole lot of control over my emotions. Every now and then, I would have a lucid moment and wonder if I was dealing fatal blows to my marriage. For the most part, though, I was immersed in my pain. I was fighting hard to survive, and anything else was just too complicated to think about.

After several months, I stopped raging and became more zombielike. Nothing really affected me one way or the other. I would laugh occasionally, but I wasn't really feeling it. I used to be very emotional. Cute puppies would make me cry. No more. I didn't feel anything for a while. My poor husband was really confused at this point. I went from raging maniac to Stepford wife. Whatever he wanted to do, fine. Whatever he didn't want to do, fine. In some ways, I think it was worse for him. He had no idea what I was feeling. What he didn't understand is that I wasn't feeling anything. I felt dead inside and was only going through the motions. It was just too much effort to feel anything. So I didn't. Maybe it was a layer of protection; I don't know. There was no way I could ever go through the type of pain I felt when Davey died, so subconsciously, I decided to feel nothing in case something else horrific was going to happen. However, at that time, I had no idea that's what I was doing. I actually thought I was better. I wasn't crying and screaming all the time. I was pleasant to be around and would somewhat engage in life, in conversations, but I was actually numb. All the things I have described went on for the first year or so. After that first year is when I started to come around.

I have read that a lot of marriages don't survive a loss of this magnitude, and I can see why. It's very difficult to survive and deal with your grief and take care of a marriage. In fact, I don't think you can do all those things at once. I'm happy to say, I was lucky. We did survive. Once I started to have a little more control over my emotions, I understood that I needed to take better care. I learned in therapy (even though it took me an extralong time) that there were better ways to channel my feelings of anger and grief.

Once I was feeling better, I started looking at Rick differently. I will never forget how his love shined brightly for me in my time of need. I will never forget how he stood by my side through each and every horrible day, how he had my back always, and how he took care of me when I could give nothing back to him.

We've come a long way since that first year. Do we still argue? Well, sure. We're both still a bit on the stubborn side. I still don't think he has mastered sock folding. Just kidding! We have learned what is important and what is not. Before Davey's accident, I would get irritated over minor issues at times. What a waste! We have learned that, when we do have disagreements or a difference of opinion, they are just that. We have learned to cut through the crap and focus on what matters. I lost so much when I lost Davey, but I've also gained a new perspective. He has taught me that every day is precious now. Rick deserves a partner who gives back as much as he gives.

Is my marriage perfect now? Nope. It's not all puppies and white picket fences. We are real people who deal with real challenges. I have learned that we are a team, and that's how we live our lives. We have both learned so much since the accident. We know that our marriage comes first. Period. We have learned to communicate better. Most importantly, we respect each other. And we no longer sweat the small stuff.

CHAPTER

12

As I have said earlier, that first month was incredibly brutal, so brutal, in fact, that I can't recall a lot of it. In my darkest moments, though, there was a small beam of light trying to get through. That beam of light was my daughter. I was suffering immeasurably, but so was she. She was my daughter, and she needed me. It was so difficult. It's hard to describe the mind-numbing shock and pain that I was feeling. I can only describe it as living in a deep fog. I was only vaguely aware of what was going on in the world around me, and I was not able to participate in any way. The depression was so great that I just couldn't see living in a world without Davey. But Cari needed me, and I needed to find a way to be there for her.

Once we both got home after the accident, it was very hard to talk to her at first. That's completely weird to me as I love her beyond measure and we talk just about every day. Every time we got on the phone, the tears would be flowing. Both of us were reeling, and neither of us had a clue about how to get through it.

Not only was she feeling absolutely devastated, but she was also dealing with her brother's affairs. He had designated her his advocate if something happened to him. I tried to help her as much as I could, but once again, I was pretty much useless. I remember getting phone calls from his credit-card company because he had obviously missed a payment. I finally worked up the courage to tell the lady on the phone that my son had passed away. It was the first time that I said it out loud, and it was awful. It will be one of those things that will always stay with me.

It took quite a while to get his affairs straightened out, which was weird because he was young and didn't have a whole lot. It took some time, but we made sure all his bills were paid and his accounts were settled. It was suggested that we let those things go, but it was important to us that Davey leave this earth in good standing. He would have never let his bills go, and we weren't going to either, even if he wasn't here to reap those rewards.

Cari and I have always been very close, and we were even more so during this period. I had Rick, and she had her fiancé, John, but it wasn't the same. By this time, she and her dad were having some issues and were not communicating much. As with him and me, it was just too painful. We clung to each other. We poured out our hearts over and over. Screamed and cried at the unfairness of it all. It took a really long time before we could discuss everyday happenings in our phone calls.

As difficult as it was, I knew deep down that we had to keep talking and crying and feeling. It wasn't for me; I was feeling that there was no hope I would ever feel better. It was for her. I learned in therapy that tears are what heal you. In that case, I have cried enough tears to heal entire nations. Another thing that I learned in therapy is that many people cannot recover from this type of loss and they become bitter. Or they turn to drugs and alcohol to cope. Even in my worst moments, I was adamant that Cari survive this. I wanted her not to be cheated out of a life she has worked hard for and a life she deserves. She and John are planning a wedding and someday would like to have a family. Her future children deserve a mother who is fully invested in life.

So we pushed through, together. I made myself available to her 24-7. If she wanted to talk, scream, or cry, I was there. Sometimes, it was the blind leading the blind. I repeatedly encouraged her to get into grief counseling. Sometimes I felt counseling was the only thing keeping me alive, and I thought it could help her too. She did eventually get into a group therapy for people who had lost a loved one, and it made all the difference. To talk to people who understand your pain and what you are going through can make all the difference. And later, she did go to an individual counselor who was able to give her guidance to continue on her path to healing.

As a mom, we want nothing more than to shelter our kids from pain. That's not very realistic is it? Life is full of challenges, and one of our many tasks as a parent is to teach our kids how to meet those challenges head on. Can you imagine how I was feeling? My life was reeling out of control. I was deeply entrenched in the most painful thing I had ever been through, and Cari needed me. It was rough, no doubt about it. Even in my darkest moments, I knew I had to find a way for Cari and me to carry on. She was worth saving even if I had no hope of saving myself.

CHAPTER

13

My path continued this way for about a year. As I have said before, most of that year was spent going through the motions. We filled our days trying to do things that would distract us from the pain. Those distractions were just that. They were totally unimportant, and I couldn't tell you what they were. The therapist has said that is what happens to you when you are in shock and grieving in that intense and all-consuming way.

After about a year, I was reaching the point where I was tired of feeling so bad. I believe this is the moment when I started the healing process. Was it ever going to get better? I finally had a glimmer of hope that maybe it would. I learned in therapy that, over time, grief becomes less intense. I have told you how I fought it for a long time. That if I got better, I was somehow dishonoring my son. I finally realized that feeling like that was just crazy. Davey would never want us to keep suffering. Why was I so convinced that I had to hold on to the worst pain that I have ever felt? I have learned that this too is also part of the grieving process.

I was slowly starting to emerge from my fog. I was beginning to realize that I had not been there for my husband, my parents, my employer, my coworkers, or my golden retriever, Shay. I was starting to feel a little guilty. Whatever energy I did have was for Cari.

These were people who had stood by me throughout all this, and I needed to be a little more present.

Did I wake up one year later and feel miraculously better? Of course not. I was still in a lot of pain. In fact, when that fog lifted, I went backward for a bit. Without that fog covering, I was forced to deal with my new reality.

My new reality is that I had to find a way to move forward. I was still firmly entrenched in my grief, but as I mentioned earlier, I now wanted to get better. This is something that bears repeating: I believe with every fiber of my being that, if you want to survive this, you have to feel the pain. Feeling that pain and the tears is what heals you. Your brain has a way of letting you feel only what you can handle a little bit at a time. When you realize over time that your pain is a little less intense, then you understand that you are on the path to feeling better.

Feeling and grieving are not the easy path to take. The easier path is to block the pain. The easier way is to be bitter and angry about the unfairness of it all. The easier way is to immerse yourself in alcohol or abuse drugs. In the long run, I believe those things eventually become the more difficult road. Those things never allow you to heal. Those things will never allow you to feel real joy or happiness or even sadness. Those things erode your soul. Do I sound preachy? That's not my intent. I'm only talking about what I learned along the way.

As time has gone on, I would say I'm better. I will never be the person that I was before the accident, nor do I have any desire to be that person. I also believe that I'm probably as good as I'm going to get. I will never feel the same about holidays. There will always be an element of sadness about them. I have a very hard time on Davey's birthday. That day always brings on the feelings about what could have been and where he would have been in his life by now. I have come to absolutely hate the month of April; Davey died in April.

Last April, as soon as the calendar changed over to signify the beginning of the month, I could feel myself starting to slip. Everything came roaring back. It had been safely tucked into my heart, and now grief was once again rearing its ugly head. I was angry, sad, and out of control. Rick had no idea how to deal with me. I knew I was worrying my mom too, but I just didn't care. I just kept reliving the accident and the aftermath. I was going downhill fast.

I used to love April. After a long winter of looking at barren brown trees, I always have been so excited to see them come alive. I loved watching the flowers bloom and have always enjoyed all the colors of spring. No more—I was losing it.

About halfway through the month, I realized that I couldn't continue like this. I was quickly sinking into a despair that I hadn't felt in a while. I realized that, if I let myself continue down this road, I might not make it back again. I made the conscious decision to take charge of my emotions, maybe for the first time in my life. Was it easy? Um, it was not; it felt foreign. It would have been easier to do nothing and just continue my downward spiral. You want to know who made me knock it off? Davey. He would have been appalled at my gigantic helping of self-pity. And that's what it was. Feeling sorry for myself over what I had lost. Yeah, I know that I have every right to feel that way at times, but that wasn't how I wanted to live my life.

I survived April, and later during professional counseling, the therapist helped me to understand that I now had some control over my grief. We may not be able to help how we feel, but we *can* control how we react to those feelings. Now, when I slip into angry or sad emotions, I remember that I do have some control over how I want to get through it. In the old days, when I would get angry or upset, Davey used to say "Calm down, Mother" in a way that would dissolve my anger and make me laugh. That is what I kept telling myself the month of April. I could see his face, and it worked. Even now, that kid is keeping me on track!

CHAPTER

14

As I have mentioned before, after the accident, I became pretty much a completely different person. I now define my life as "before the accident" and "after the accident." The person I was before is gone, never to return. All my preconceived notions, ideas, and dreams? Gone. The things I considered important before? Trivial by comparison.

What a joke. Yes, I have always known how important my family is and how important it is to take care of your health etc. But envy over a friend's good fortune or that someone you know is better off financially or has a bigger home? Really? Those things just don't matter to me anymore, and I'm ashamed to admit they ever did.

One of the things I kept thinking about after the accident is that Davey is watching over me now. Even in my deepest grief, I wanted to make him proud. It has become very important to me to live a life that honors his memory. It is what fuels me every day. Did I just wake up one day a most marvelous individual? Not at all. And it's not as if I lived a life of crime and deception before; I simply decided I could do better. I have been on a journey of self-discovery ever since. It is something I will continue for the rest of my life.

One of the first things I decided to do was to reach out to people more. After the accident, I was stunned at the outpouring of love and support from my friends, coworkers, and neighbors. They started a GoFundMe account to help with funeral expenses. They coordinated meals so that we wouldn't have to worry about cooking and would be fed. They checked on me regularly. They made me get up and walk in the morning so that my puppy could get exercise. Cari's friends stepped up and helped with the funeral arrangements. The love we felt from Davey's friends and coworkers astounded me—I just had no idea. Had I ever reached out like that? The sad news is I had not. Yes, I contributed to donation funds and signed cards but had never reached out in a personal way. It made me realize I could, and should, do better.

The accident was in April, and when December rolled around, I did not have the heart or desire to even think about Christmas. Celebrating the holiday was something I just couldn't contemplate. It seemed ludicrous to me to put up a tree and pretend that I cared about gift giving and all the things associated with the holidays. I wasn't alone—nobody in my family felt up to it.

I started thinking that, while I had no desire to celebrate Christmas, maybe we could do something to make someone else's Christmas better. I decided to talk to Cari and my mom and dad, thinking that maybe we could do something together. I had no idea how to even go about something like this. Davey loved kids, so I really wanted to do something that would brighten some little one's holiday. A friend put me in touch with a wonderful lady at our local elementary school. She knew just the family in our little community who needed some help. They had four small children and had fallen on hard times. We decided to do what we could do to help them have a nice holiday. It gave me a little break from my constant sadness and helped me focus on others who were also struggling, albeit in a different way. I actually enjoyed the shopping and wrapping, and it did my aching heart good to see those happy little faces! I could see Davey giving me his signature two thumbs up.

For our holiday, we didn't exchange gifts, but we did quietly celebrate with a nice dinner. I was still completely numb on the inside, but it made me feel good that we had carried out something special and that I survived the first Christmas without my baby. The first holidays after losing a loved one are usually the most difficult to bear.

After the first year, I was starting to feel a little bit better, and I started reaching out to others in small ways. I would often give a little bit of money to a disabled gentleman who was always in the grocery-store parking lot of the small town in which I lived. I'm ashamed to admit that I never took the time to really talk to him. One day I decided to change that. You know what I discovered? He was the sweetest, kindest man! He had fallen on hard times and was trying to raise a young daughter and keep his home. Because of his disability, he was having trouble finding work. I continued to talk with him and give him a little money when I could. He eventually moved to another state to be closer to family and for a job opportunity.

I've discovered that small acts of kindness revive and nourish my spirit. Sometimes I will give the cashier at the drive-through a little extra to treat the person behind me in line. Maybe that person will pay it forward. If Rick and I are out eating and we see first responders or members of the military, we like to pay for their meal, just a small way of thanking them for their service. I hope, one day after I retire, to do some volunteer work around the community.

These types of things are not major. I will never run a charity or head a philanthropy group. Reaching out in small ways is something that I can do and will continue to do. I want to give back to a community that was there for me in my darkest hour.

You know what else I have discovered? That smiling at people, saying hello to strangers, and looking folks in the eye when you talk to them make a huge difference. I guess I just never paid attention to that type of stuff before, things like holding doors open or assisting an elderly person in the grocery store. Basic manners, you say? That is true, and it's not like I was mean and rude and ignored everyone. I had a bad habit of being in my head a lot and not being attentive to others. Now, I choose to pay attention every time I am out. Those are the things that make people realize they matter, and it really takes little to no effort. Recently, I was with Cari, and I noticed she has this incredible way of making the people she speaks with feel like the most important person in her life. We should all have a little bit of her positive outlook. Even after what she has been through, she manages to reach out to people in a way that is positive and exuberant.

As I have mentioned before, my priorities have completely changed. I am, by nature, shy and on the quiet side. I have always been content to live my life on the sidelines, one of the many things about me that frustrated Davey. He was always encouraging me to find my voice, to find my passion. I was never going to do those things; I was not an active participant in my own life.

Always afraid to rock the boat, always afraid that someone may judge me. That was the old me in my "before life." I was not honoring my son by not being true to my values and the things I believe in because someone may judge me. My attitude now? I have been learning and still have a long way to go, but I am finding my voice. I do have opinions and values and beliefs. It's okay for me to stand up for what I believe. It's okay if others want to disagree or judge me. I have often said that losing Davey is the worst thing that has ever happened to me. Someone judging my actions hardly makes a blip on my radar anymore. However, I think there was a period in which I was going too far. I was angry and just spouting off whatever I wanted. If you'll remember, I had been clear after the accident that living life in angry mode was not what I wanted. But for a while there, I couldn't control what came out of my mouth. It was Cari who reminded me that I had never been that person and I needed to tone it down a bit. She was absolutely right. I was appalled when it finally dawned on me that I was being rude and taking out my anger on people just because I was in pain. Yikes! Not exactly honoring your son there, huh, Deb?

I am finally learning to like myself, flaws and all, and, more importantly, trust myself. I am learning that my needs and concerns are valid. I have never ever given myself that validity before. Now, I want to clarify that I will never be the "guns a-blazing" type of person. You will never hear me screaming my opinions from the rooftop or posting them all over social media. But I am quietly discovering that I can make a difference, even if it's a small one.

My therapist has told me these things are a blessing. As I have told you before, at first I was outraged. I can just never see a scenario in which losing my baby will ever be a blessing. But as time has passed, I have more of an understanding of what she was talking about. I have learned what is important. I like to think that the things I have learned are a gift from my son. Would I have preferred another way to receive these gifts? Of course, but this is my life now.

Since I have started to come around, I have spent a lot of time observing people. We live in a time in which many people think it's acceptable to behave badly, whether it's being rude to others or the vitriol that is spewed on social media. I'm having a hard time with it all. I wonder what causes someone to be so awful. I really don't understand why some of those people enjoy being ugly, with no regard as to how some of their statements may be taken. I do know that everyone at one time or another is fighting battles, battles that are none of my business. I truly don't want to judge others. Losing a child is so horrific. I've had to fight hard not to become that ugly person. I have to work every day to not be bitter. And it takes practice, let me tell you. Just the other day, I was going down the highway where the speed limit was sixty-five and happened to get behind someone going forty. My first thought was "*Dude!* Move it!" Then I remembered that it's better to be kind and maybe he had a problem with his car. I just try to be aware of my actions while realizing that I will always be a work in progress and will screw up on a regular basis.

Reading this over, I realize it sounds like I want to live in a fairy-tale world where everyone is nice and cute puppies are everywhere. It *would* be nice, however, it's not reality. For me, though, honoring Davey's memory means striving to be a better person.

My hope in sharing my journey is that you too find a way to survive your loss. It's a terrible thing to have to live with, and for me, finding small ways to help others makes it a little more tolerable.

CHAPTER

15

This part of my story is probably not for everyone, but it is an integral part of my journey. As I have alluded to earlier, I believe in the afterlife and always have. It's never been an issue for me; it's always been a part of who I am. Until the accident, I had never thought twice about those beliefs. But, as with every other part of my life, I started to question those beliefs. I started wondering if what I was seeing or feeling was just a way to make myself feel better.

I would like to acknowledge that everyone has his or her own belief system in place. I also know that what I believe doesn't coincide with some religious beliefs or with those who have no religious beliefs. There are people who are just naturally skeptical. All those things are okay. I am not on a mission here to convince anyone to change his beliefs. I am only sharing my story.

I have had what they call "dream visitations" for as long as I can remember. In fact, I had no idea that not everyone has them. I have had vivid dreams from friends and loved ones who have passed over. I don't have them all the time; it's only occasionally. During my reading about the afterlife, I learned that those visitation dreams are a favorite way for our loved ones to visit us.

After we returned to Arizona following the accident, I became obsessed with reading everything I could about the afterlife. I probably read seventy-five books. I was searching for answers. I wanted to know exactly what happens when you die. I wanted to make sure Davey was okay in heaven.

One of the very best books I have read and still refer to often is *Questions about the Afterlife*, written by Bob Olson. He is a private investigator who has spent the last fifteen years researching the afterlife. He also does an Afterlife TV podcast. The book was so comforting to me when I desperately needed it, and I still listen to his podcasts. He is a wonderful person who has been such a help to me.

The books that I read all basically said the same thing. Your body may die, but your spirit never does. I may not have my son here in the physical sense, but it brings me great comfort to know he is all around me. I would think that would be a comfort to anyone who has suffered a loss of someone they love.

I have seen Davey many times in my dreams, and I always feel he is trying to give me a message. Problem is the blonde in me doesn't always get what the message is for a while. They do seem to make sense when the time is right. I feel like he is guiding me, and that is one of the reasons I strive to be better. Just a few days ago, I dreamt he was wrapping my fingers around a keyboard. I had been feeling that maybe there wasn't enough in my story to make a difference and maybe he was telling me otherwise. I have had many variations of a dream in which he is taking me back to the house that we lived in while raising the kids. In the dreams, we are in various stages of moving out of the house and packing up in a big moving van. He is always at different ages in these dreams. I always wake up feeling that he is trying to tell me to let go of my past and to start my new beginning.

Shortly after Rick and I got together, I had a vivid dream in which my ex-mother-in-law, who had passed several years prior, was leading me into a white building. She was dressed completely in white, and the inside of the building was white as well. We rounded a corner, and there was Rick's first wife. She was sitting in a hospital bed, and her hair and makeup were done. What did she want? Well, she gave me the biggest hug. It felt magical. I woke up thinking that she had just given her blessing for Rick and me to have a life together. These visitation dreams are so vivid, so real. I remember expressions and colors; in fact, I pretty much remember everything about them. I am a big dreamer, and some of my dreams are just plain weird—my own mother sometimes thinks I'm a freak! But most of those dreams do not have the same visual clarity as a visitation dream has, and I have usually forgotten them by morning.

Are these dreams open to interpretation? Absolutely! I have asked myself over and over if I am somehow just making these dreams up, even though I have been having these dreams my entire life. I have brought this up in therapy, oh, about a million times. My therapist continues to patiently tell me that maybe it's time for me to take that leap of faith. I had always believed it before; why was I questioning those beliefs now? She has also told me that she has seen and heard too much not to believe there is an afterlife. It always goes back to my thinking that, if I allowed myself to feel better about any of what happened, then I wasn't doing the whole grief thing correctly. I can't tell you what a long time I spent trying to convince myself that, if I felt better, then I was betraying my son. What a doofus I was!

I also "see" people. I know it makes me sound like a weirdo, and maybe I am! I will be going about my day, and all of a sudden, I will have a vision of someone. I never know who these people are. For example, one day I was working, sitting at my computer. Out of the blue, I had a vision of a very pretty blond woman lying on her side, propped up on her elbow. She was wearing a blue satin evening gown, and she had a tiara on her head. She had long blond hair and chubby cheeks. She had the biggest smile on her face, and I have no idea who she was. Just recently, I have seen a couple dressed in clothes maybe from the seventies. They are standing on a blanket in a park, and they both have their arms crossed. He had curly brown hair, and she had long blond hair. Sitting on the blanket at their feet was a small child. They have blank stares on their face. Again, no idea who they are. I also get visions of a man who is clearly from the eighteen hundreds. I can tell by what he is wearing and his bushy sideburns. He is always staring at me, and I see him often. A long-ago relative? Maybe, but those bushy sideburns can't possibly be from my side of the family!

I did not have these visions before the accident, or if I did, I paid no attention to them. But now, I have spent a lot of time healing, reading, and trying to find clarity to what happened and what my life is now. Some would say my vibration has been raised, and I am more open now to these things. I am used to them now; however, in the beginning I was startled by them. For those of you not familiar with the term "raising your vibration," it means that you are moving from an emotional place that is hard with thick walls and not a lot of flexibility. It's what fear and pain and anger do. Raising your vibration is to push through those thick walls, open your heart, and follow your truths. I believe that raising your vibration allows you to move forward, to experience emotional growth.

I also see Davey on occasion. The other day, I was acting in a ridiculous manner, and all of a sudden, there he was. He had his arms crossed, was shaking his head with a bemused expression on his face. Every time Cari or I see him, he is always surrounded by the most beautiful blue color. We now always refer to blue as Davey blue.

Once Rick and I were at a huge car show in Phoenix. For some reason, I felt compelled to look behind me. There he was. He was walking with a short blond girl. He had on his favorite gray shorts and white T-shirt. His keys were clipped onto his belt loop as always, and he had his favorite sunglasses on. He looked at me and smiled, and then he was gone. Nobody loved cars more than Davey did, so where else would you expect him to be? That vision only lasted a few seconds, but once again, he was showing me that he is always with me.

There have also been some other things that I have seen and felt. Shortly after the accident, when I was contemplating the tattoo, I was working at my desk. My arm wasn't moving, and I felt my bracelet move. Even in that fog of despair that I was feeling, I knew this was a sure sign from Davey that he wanted me to get that tattoo. It sits on the inside of my wrist where that bracelet always lies.

Cari and I have always thought that hummingbirds were a visit from him. On occasion, one will fly right by my office window and hang out right in front of the window for a few seconds. Cari sees them a lot more than I do. My therapist recently moved her office, and the office has a large window. About a month ago, during a session, I looked at the window, and there was a hummingbird, just hanging out at the window. It was awesome!

I also have visits from yellow butterflies. I spend a lot of time in my backyard as I have a tennis-ball-obsessed golden retriever that insists on me throwing balls. I have seen several butterflies. Once there was a particularly pesky yellow butterfly that kept flying all around me. I said out loud, "If you are Davey, please let me know." Do you know that butterfly flew right up to my face and stayed there flapping its wings for a bit? It did my heart good.

One thing that has happened is one of my most treasured memories. It was Christmas 2015. By this time, it had been a little over a year and a half since the accident. I had a houseful of people. I didn't really feel up to doing the whole Christmas thing again that year, but my stepdaughter and her family were visiting from Alaska. Rick doesn't see them as often as he would like as it is super expensive to fly in and out of Juneau. She has four lively boys, and I thought it would be good for us to have them there. Cari and John were also there.

It was the night before Christmas Eve, and everyone had gone to the store except for Cari, John and me. Cari and I were in my bedroom, sitting on the bed, talking and quietly crying about how much we missed Davey and that Christmas was never going to be the same. A few minutes later, the three of us were sitting in the living room. All of a sudden, the overhead light in the ceiling fan, and the lamp right beside where I was sitting flicked on and off three times.

Because we had a houseful of people staying there, it seemed every light in the house was on. No other lights made any movement. There was no storm outside or any other reason to explain what had happened. It was Davey letting us know that he was there for Christmas after all. Having that visitation and a loud, rambunctious Christmas was just what the doctor ordered.

I am aware that there are plenty of skeptics out there, including members of my own family. They say, quite reasonably, that there can be simple explanations for the things that have happened. Including the fact that I could be bonkers. All that is true, well, except for the fact that I am not completely off my rocker yet. Even if there are plausible explanations for everything that I have described, how do you know it's not Davey? It goes back to what I have been taught in therapy. Why not take that leap of faith? There are signs everywhere. You just have to be open to those signs. I have read over and over that our loved ones want to give us signs from the afterlife. They want you to know they're all right. Don't you want that too? There is absolutely no proof that there is not an afterlife.

CHAPTER

16

Since I have been diving into getting all the knowledge I can about the afterlife, I decided that I wanted to get a reading. What if I could connect with Davey? How awesome would that be? There were other things about the afterlife that I had questions about, so over the course of two years, I went to a past-life regressionist, a psychic consultant, and a psychic medium. I found them all so interesting. I will tell you, however, that Rick was totally skeptical and thought I was wasting money. He's one of those people who like proof.

During my research after the accident, I was introduced to past-life regression. This is not something that I had ever heard of. The theory is that your spirit has lived many, many lives and that you can tap into those lives by going through a past-life regression. There was a part of me that was really unsure about this, but the bigger part of me was intrigued and wanted to find out more. I kept thinking that Davey, Cari, and I had such a bond. Was it possible that we have had that bond for a very long time?

I found this wonderful past-life regressionist in Sedona, about an hour from where I live. I was excited but nervous wondering what I was getting myself into and if I was wasting my money.

My mom and I drove to Sedona the day of the appointment. She had my mom wait outside and then explained the situation and what was about to happen. I would be hypnotized and then walk down a hall with several doors. I had to open any one of the doors of my choosing. I had never been hypnotized before and was suddenly a little bit fearful. What the heck was I getting myself into? I even thought to myself that I might not even fall for the whole hypnosis thing.

Well, she did hypnotize me, and I did open one of those doors. The first thing I saw were men riding horses, carrying long swords, and wearing some type of armor. That only lasted a few seconds, and then I was lying in a bed. I have no idea how I knew the person in the bed was me. I was lying there very sad. Apparently, my family home had burned to the ground, and my entire family had perished in the fire. I could see the house had been set fire by a man wearing all black on a horse. The regressionist then asked me if I could identify the face of the arsonist. It was somebody that I know very well in this life.

The next thing I saw was this same man (me) in a house with a blond lady who appeared to be my wife. Her name was Leonora, and my name was Clancy. I looked out the window, and there were twin boys playing in the yard. I instinctively knew that one of those boys was my Davey!

My next vision was Clancy assisting injured soldiers in the Civil War. He was in North Carolina, and he was a surgeon taking care of Confederate soldiers. Now, as anyone who knows me will tell you, I have been obsessed with North Carolina since I was a young girl. When I finally did go for the first time in 2010, I stepped off the plane and felt like I was home and that I had been there before. Well, apparently, I have been there before! Working beside me with those soldiers was a nurse. My mom! Only she wasn't my mom then. I also was able to see Rick riding a horse through the town, and Cari was my neighbor. The session ended after I saw that Clancy had lived a long life and had his family by his side when he died from some type of chest malady.

The best part of the whole session? When it was over and I was coming out of my hypnotic state, there was Davey! Again, surrounded by blue and he had his arms outstretched. That moment is something I will never forget.

A couple of interesting things I got from this reading? Aside from the whole North Carolina thing? My career has always been in health care. I was a nurse before I started doing billing.

The other? Cari has always wanted to name her first little girl Eleanor. The woman that was married to Clancy was named Leonora. Very close.

The next reading I had was with a psychic consultant who is involved in prebirth planning. The theory here is that your life was planned out for you before you were born with your spirit and your spirit guides. That you intentionally "sign up" for certain challenges when you return to earth. I was intrigued by this because why on earth would I sign up for something as horrific as losing a child? I really wanted to explore this.

We did a phone reading. All she asked for was my first name and date of birth. We then talked briefly about what I was looking for. She then asked for Davey's first name and date of birth. She asked for a few moments of silence while she gathered information from the spirit.

Davey came through right away. She said she could feel a very strong connection between Davey and me and that his spirit was all around me. She wanted to know exactly what I needed from him. I explained that I wanted to make sure he was okay in the spirit world. She said that he was finally healed. This is what she told me.

The first thing she said is that she saw a little bit of a fire around his accident. I told her that I had no knowledge of a fire. I had chosen not to get every detail of the accident. She kept saying that the engine looked like it had a small fire at the time of impact.

She then said he had a huge smile on his face, and he kept saying, "I'm okay. I'm okay!" He said that spiritually he was healed and that what he set out to do in this lifetime had been achieved and that I was a direct part of that. He went on to tell a very interesting story. He related that, three lifetimes ago, he purposely chose a life of depression and loneliness as a way to enhance his spiritual growth in future lifetimes. He was an uneducated man living away from society and depended on hunting to survive. He was acquainted with two men who also lived nearby. One day he was out hunting, and he heard them. He found the first one and shot him with his bow and arrow in the chest. He then hunted down the second man and shot him in the back of the leg. The man died six days later from an infection, and it was a slow and agonizing death.

After he passed from that lifetime, he was going through a life review and saw that what he had done to those men was wrong. He asked the spirits of the two men he had harmed if they would forgive him. They were not able to grant him that forgiveness until this most recent life. It was decided that Davey would die an unexpected, violent death just like they had. They were the two men in the car that hit him.

He went on to say that he is healed now, he is forgiven, and he is happy. That his most recent journey was a journey of self-awareness, healthy self-centeredness, and perseverance. He was able to achieve goals in his most recent lifetime that he was never able to do in his previous lives. He now feels such a spiritual connection to all things, something he has never been able to do in any of his previous lives. That because he went through that karmic lesson, he became emotionally balanced and more adaptive to new situations.

She then asked me if I had any questions. I remember telling her that it was a bit rough hearing that he had been capable of killing someone. She then told me that Davey was telling her that he was able to heal because of my love and guidance. She said that she also saw me in a couple of Davey's previous lives, and I was guiding him and teaching him in those lives as well. We then discussed my past-life regression where I was a doctor and he was my son. That teaching and guidance were a part of my life then too.

She then said she saw Davey hold his hands to his chest and then opened his hands and arms wide and a yellow butterfly came out. He then said, "I'm happy, Mother!" He said *mother* just like he used to say when he was making a point.

The third reading happened just recently. I heard about a medium who sounded very interesting. So I set up an appointment. All I was interested in was Davey coming through.

The medium is in Massachusetts, so we did a phone reading. Right away, things started happening.

Before I tell you what happened it's important you know I did not give her any information beforehand. She knew nothing about me at all except my name and phone number.

The first spirit that came through was a "grandmother." The medium said her name was Lon or Bon—Bonnie! That was my maternal grandmother's name. She died when I was a child, and when she said the name, I wasn't sure if it was even correct. She and my mom had a complicated relationship and had been estranged at the time of her death. Her message? She wanted my mom to know that she was looking out for her and was going to help her with healing for an upcoming surgery. My mom was scheduled to have eye surgery the following week. What the heck? There was no way the medium could have known that.

The next spirit that came through was my uncle, my mom's brother. He died twenty or so years ago from a heart attack. The medium said that he died from "something in the chest." Bingo! What he said next floored me. He said that he was the one who helped Davey cross over. Davey was a small child when my uncle died. I would have never in a million years thought he was the one who would be there. The medium then asked if my uncle smoked. Of course he did. He was always a wise ass, a prankster, someone who really never grew up. Yet he was there to help my baby cross over.

Finally, Davey showed up! The first thing the medium said to me was "Tell Ricky I said hi." I could not believe it! My kids and I have always called my husband Ricky. Everyone else calls him Rick. How could she have known that?!

Then she brought up Davey's work boots. Remember my telling you about the boots that I saw on the front porch when we went to California? Those boots. I was so shocked. She then told me that Davey wants me to put a picture or drawing of those boots on the cover of my book.

Surrounded by a bluish-green color. I thought to myself, *He's talking about our Davey blue. These are things she couldn't possibly know about.*

She then said that Davey wanted us to know his death was an accident. That there was no malicious intent by anyone involved. That he knew deep down his life would not be long.

He then asked that I reach out to my ex-husband. Davey said that this has taken a terrible toll on him and he is suffering alone. I have not done so as of yet; there are some painful unresolved things between us, but again, I have no desire to disappoint my son.

The medium then said that she saw Davey holding an over-weight, older yellow dog. My Missy!

She was my first golden retriever, who had died at age twelve. I miss her terribly. She was with Davey. He also relayed that his dog Maggie was with him and she, in fact, did die of a broken heart. Just like we had suspected.

I can see where one would be totally skeptical about what I experienced at the first two readings I attended. I completely get it, because some of it I have trouble believing myself. Although in both readings there were some things that made sense to me. Davey had been on a journey of self-discovery for a very long time, and the readings reflected that. I get that there was some stuff that sounded generalized, that they could have been talking about anyone. There is no proof of any of it, and you need to take that leap of faith, I guess.

But the third reading? Holy crap, if you don't believe what she told me, then you probably don't believe in the afterlife. She knew too many details that have not been made public. I say that like I'm some famous Kardashian-type celebrity who posts what she had for breakfast! That could not be further from the truth. What I should have said is that she knew things she could not possibly know without knowing me personally. She talked about how honest and straightforward Davey was. How funny he was.

What I learned from those readings is the afterlife truly does exist. Even though I had had dream visitations before and had always believed that, when Davey died, all my beliefs about everything were thrown into turmoil. That's why I started reading so many books on the subject. That's why I went through the readings. My beliefs are back now to what they were before the accident. Davey is with me every minute of every day, and he is watching out for me, for all the people he loved. That last reading restored my faith.

The last thing she said to me? "Your book will be published." Really? Cool! If you are reading this, then you know she was correct. I did not mention to her that I was writing a book until she said that.

CHAPTER

17

Even more compelling is Cari's story with regard to Davey and the afterlife. I told you earlier that they have always had an extraordinary relationship that continues to this day. They just have always understood each other from day one.

After the accident, Cari also started having visions of him almost immediately. I asked her once if it freaked her out at all when they started. I don't recall that death and the afterlife were something that I had ever really discussed with either of my kids before. She said that, maybe for a minute, she was unsure of what was happening. Then she said she knew instinctively that Davey was there. She does not very often get dream visitations from him as I do. He just appears to her. He also likes to tease her as he had often done his whole life. He will open the door to her guest bedroom when she has just closed it. Sometimes he will turn the light on in the guest room just for fun.

I realize while writing this that I make it sound like it's all perfectly normal stuff because, to us, it is. When Davey was here, he always looked out for us. He's still doing that. He was always the most technologically savvy of us all, always up-to-date on the latest advances. It makes sense to me that he is continuing that in heaven.

For the longest time after the accident, Cari would see him all the time. He would jog beside her as she was taking her morning run; he would sit beside her when she meditated. He would always seem to know when she needed him. We would be talking about Davey, and she would instantly see him.

She talks to him a lot. He does not verbally communicate with her, but he does telepathically communicate with her. He will shake his head yes or no to her questions. He will shake his head in amusement at her antics. Cari can be what we lovingly refer to as ridiculous. The things I adore about her, the things that make her unique, are also the things that can drive me crazy about her too! He will also push his hands down when he wants her to calm down. I can hear him now, "Cari, calm *down*!" It was a phrase he was quite fond of telling us both.

Sometimes I will be talking to her about something and will mention that I will love his opinion. For instance, I was concerned about writing this book and putting things out there that are private. I didn't want to write about anyone and have that person react unfavorably. I also worried about sharing too much about Davey's struggles or the pain that we have endured. It isn't easy to put everything out there. While we were talking, Davey communicated through Cari that it was important for me to put it all out there. Everything. So you can thank Davey.

He also seems to communicate with one of Cari's dogs, a lab named Rogue. Cari can always tell when Rogue senses Davey. If you ask him where Uncle Davey is, he always looks over at Davey's picture on the wall.

As time has gone on and Cari has begun the healing process, he goes to her less and less. She does feel his presence, however, she just doesn't see him as much. When she is overly stressed by life, she doesn't see him as much because her vibration just isn't that high. He still seems to know when we need him, however. We know he was here more in the beginning because we were both reeling.

Once, Cari asked Davey if he missed us. His response? It was a big, fat no. He doesn't miss us because he is with us all the time. He always knows what's going on in our lives. He likes it like that. He will sometimes sit with his grandpa in the den while he is watching TV. Or he will be out in the back with his grandma while she is out gardening. He indicated to Cari that he loves keeping tabs on us all at the same time. He also loves that he is helping us, guiding us. I have always believed that you have to listen to your gut when contemplating a decision. Now, I know that feeling is him. I am always aware that, everything I do or every decision that I need to make, he is with me, guiding me.

Sometimes Cari will see him only briefly, or he doesn't come in clearly. But lately, there have been a few life-changing events in play for her, and she has been seeing him more. She has been planning the wedding and buying a new house, and she just knows he's there beside her, guiding her in the right direction. I have been seeing him more lately as well. Recently, she and I were texting about whether she and John should buy a house they had seen and fallen in love with, and there he was. Clear as day. He was wearing a blue T-shirt and had his favorite hat on. He was shaking his head vigorously up and down to our questions. I loved seeing him, and I hope for more of those visits even though they usually last only for a few seconds.

Davey has also communicated to Cari that he knew his life would not be a long one. That is still so hard for me to think about. But he has also reassured her he is completely happy now. He has both his dogs with him, along with my dog Missy. He says the best feeling of all is that he is free. Free of the things he struggled with for most of his life. Free from complicated relationships that he could not fix. Free from pain, sadness, and worry.

He has also communicated to Cari that one of his jobs in heaven is to assist people as they pass over. Recently, John's grandfather passed away. Cari saw Davey greet him and thank him for his service. He was retired from the military. Cari saw this before she was able to get to the hospital and before she was told that Grandpa had passed away. Now, occasionally, when she is meditating, she will see Davey on one side and Grandpa on the other.

One day while she was meditating, Davey came through loudly and clearly. It seems he wanted to share with her some of the souls he had come across while in heaven. He spoke about a very dear friend of mine who had passed away a few years ago. He has been with her, and she recently came to me in a dream. He mentioned that he had also been with his paternal grandma, Nana. When he communicates, he does it at lightning speed. Cari said it was happening so fast that she thinks she missed some of what he was telling her.

Does this sound crazy? I'm sure to a nonbeliever it does. I assure you, neither Cari nor I are loony. We consider ourselves lucky to get these communications.

CHAPTER

18

Several months back, Cari and I were having an unusually tough time when we were together. There just seemed to be a lot of tension in the room. Nothing unusual for a mother and daughter, you say? Well, we are incredibly close and don't usually have much to argue about. But something was off. I went to spend the weekend with her, and we got into a big argument. There was yelling and tears, and I even decided to cut my visit short. A few weekends before that, we had another big argument when I was there to shop for wedding dresses. We decided to calm the heck down and hash it out.

Cari had spent the last several months planning her wedding. I was so excited about the wedding! Her fiancé, John, is a wonderful young man. But for some reason, she had been reluctant to fully engage in the planning of her wedding. I was getting irritated at what I considered to be her sometimes flippant behavior. I wanted her and John's day to be special, a wedding that reflected the love they have for each other. She finally admitted that she just didn't want to have a wedding without Davey there. She was feeling incredibly guilty about that because she wanted it to be special for John. Davey had always talked about how much he wanted to get married and have a family. Cari never wanted those things before she met John, and for some reason, she felt guilty. After his accident, her priorities changed. She also knows that Davey would never want her to give up her happiness because those things didn't happen for him.

I knew deep down why she was feeling the way she was, but I just couldn't go there. The thought of Davey not being there was just too painful to contemplate. My head was aware that he wasn't going to be there, but my heart was just not able to follow. Was that the healthy thing to do? Try to avoid the issue all together? Probably not. We talked a long time about it and realized our feelings are our feelings. We've been to hell and back. We have to continue on our path of healing, and we have to make sure we talk this stuff through. Holding things in until your head explodes is probably not the healthiest option. It for sure isn't, especially when your head does explode, because, well, that could be messy.

Another reason we were arguing, I think, is that, when we were together, it just brought everything front and center. All the memories of our lives together and the memories of the accident and aftermath were just right there in our faces. When we weren't together, we could safely return to our cocoons. We have had to learn to recognize when we are having these moments and face them head-on. And that's what we have done. I am happy to report things are relatively back to normal.

Since I started writing this, the wedding has taken place, last weekend, to be exact. It was a crazy week leading up to the big day, and Cari and I didn't really have a whole lot of time to think about the fact that it was going to happen without Davey. We both knew he would be there in spirit, but it's not the same, you know? When I would have a moment to myself and I would allow myself to go there, the tears would flow. I was feeling torn. This was my baby's wedding day. I didn't want to show her my tears. This was going to be a celebration, and I didn't want my sadness to hinder her joy.

The wedding was absolutely magical. I did cry, quite a bit. For Cari and for Davey. It's a hard thing to explain, the feelings that I was having. Absolute joy for my daughter and such sorrow for my son, At *exactly* the same time. I think the toughest part for me was when she walked down the aisle. She was so beautiful, and Davey was supposed to be there by her side. She and John got married in a church, and the ceremony was so full of love and joy. We as a family had never been particularly religious, but it is something that Cari and I have both explored since the accident. We have found that it's comforting for us now.

The reception was loud and fun, exactly the way they wanted it. There were several people who reached out to me, knowing that I was having a bit of a struggle at times. Her matron of honor gave the most heartfelt speech, and she included Davey in her speech. I was sobbing over my mashed potatoes. I told Cari later that I was so in awe of the people that she and John have surrounded themselves with. One of those so-called blessings from the accident is knowing that you no longer have time for drama or bullshit. They have good, supportive people in their lives, and it makes me happy for their future.

I made it through the wedding, and my heart is full of joy. I knew going in that I was going to have some trouble. I did, but I think I handled it better than I have in the past. These moments can be tough. The whole family together celebrating something special. He would have been a huge part of the day, and his absence was felt immensely.

Cari remained calm and relaxed the whole day. She did her best to make sure everyone knew how happy she was they had come to celebrate her and John's day. I asked her later how she did it all with such grace. She said Davey was with her the whole day, keeping her calm. She felt him everywhere she went. When the reception was coming to a close, she had a vision of Davey handing her off to John. Oh boy, more tears. Then she made me laugh. She said the look on Davey's face was priceless. "She's your problem now, John." That sounds just like something Davey would say!

When we got home, I was completely drained emotionally. I was not going to let Cari down on her day. I pulled it together and had a wonderful day. Yes, I had several rough moments, and today sucks, but tomorrow I know I will start to feel better and will be able to better reflect about what a truly wonderful day it was. I also know I did right by both of my babies. After all, they deserve no less.

CHAPTER

19

It has now been a little over three years since the accident. I would love to tell you that I have completely healed from losing Davey, but that would be a lie. I will never completely heal; I've said this before and I'll say it again: I feel like I'm probably as good as I am going to get.

There are days when life is relatively normal and I don't feel so sad. There are also days when I feel overwhelmed by despair. There are still days when I am going about my day and think to myself that I haven't heard from Davey yet today. And then I remember. There are days when I remember something funny he said, and it makes me smile. There are other days when those same memories make me sad. Because those memories are all I have left. There are days when I hear one of his favorite songs and I get that sickening feeling in my gut. Other days, those same songs will make me feel closer to him.

I recently had a dream. Davey was the center of that dream. In it, he came back to me! We were running around, trying to find his clothes. He was also trying to get his job back. He was told that his job was no longer available. He was so upset his employer did not hold his position open. When I woke up, my heart was filled with joy. He was here! The last three years had just been a horrible nightmare. And then I realized the truth. My nightmare was to continue. It seemed incredibly cruel to me. I had a rough time for a few days.

There are times when memories of Davey just pop into my head. Sometimes I laugh out loud at a memory of him being funny. I remember every bit of his face and his expressions and the sound of his voice. I remember his giant bear hugs, which made me feel safe. I remember his pranks and his exasperation at his sister and me at times. I recall his despair at times. I remember how unfair it seemed our situation was, that we were not able to spend as much time together as we would have liked, and the tears when we had to be separated again.

I remember his texting me once to tell me that he had something very important to discuss with me. He was so sorry that he had not had the courage to tell me this before. By this time, I was starting to freak out. And wondering why he couldn't just call and talk to me if it was so important. His confession? He told me he was the Batman. He thought this was so funny. I, on the other hand, wanted to smack him.

I remember how nervous he was waiting to find out if he got the job and his absolute joy when he landed that last job. His first day jitters. He called me at five o'clock in the morning, already on his way, as he didn't want to be late. He and I had that in common. Being late is just not in our DNA. However, forty-five minutes early was a bit much!

I still and will probably struggle with things. Not every day, of course, but nonetheless, those struggles are lurking, waiting for a trigger to bring them to the forefront again. A perfect example? The wedding. It's a hard thing, losing someone that you love more than life. It's hard to survive that loss. It's hard to reevaluate who you were and whom you've become. And it's a struggle to somehow meet those two people in the middle.

I have had to learn so much about myself that I never really paid attention to before. I had no idea before the accident that I could survive something so horrific. Yet I'm still standing here. I have had a few well-meaning people who have said to me that they don't know how I could survive what happened, that they would never survive something like that if it happened to them. I've often wondered what they were trying to communicate. It's like a very backhanded compliment. Just something I have pondered.

The fact that I survived tells me I'm a lot stronger than I could have ever imagined. I have had a rough time on a few occasions in my life, but nothing like this. I survived a bad marriage. I left the marriage depressed and unsure of anything. The end of a marriage is like a death in a way. You have to grieve that loss and your part in the failure of that marriage. It took me a long time to heal from that pain. Then I met Rick. He loves me in a way that gave me the freedom to find myself and learn all over how to trust. And then I lost it all again. I was once again thrown into a turmoil that made my previous years seem like a cakewalk. I have learned that he is truly one of the best things that have ever happened to me. I have learned that I have taken him for granted in the past. I have mentioned that I used to get upset over things that were just not that important. Have I completely let go of those irritations? Well, no, but I no longer sweat the stupid stuff. What I do know is I can never repay him or love him enough for the love and support he has given me through all this.

I have learned that every day is a gift, and I'm not going to waste another minute on things that just don't matter to me. Like TV, for instance. I used to be so invested in my favorite shows. Now, yes, I still watch on occasion, but it sure doesn't mean anything to me any longer.

It's hard to explain the journey of self-discovery and reevaluating one's life. My eyes have been opened to so much since the accident, not all of it bad. I have mentioned before how much I have learned about the kindness and generosity of others. I have learned that returning some of those kindnesses that were shown to me in my darkest hour makes me feel better and gives my life more purpose.

I have learned to never take the people in my life for granted. That even though I lost Davey, I have mentioned how incredibly blessed I am for having been given him and Cari. As I have mentioned about a million times, they are the greatest gift of all. How lucky I am to have incredibly supportive parents and the greatest golden retriever on the planet. How many times did I lie on her and cry my eyes out while she just let me and licked my tears in her effort to comfort me?

I have learned that it's really important to notice and enjoy the simpler things in life. Being insanely busy and stressed means that you miss out on a lot of those simple pleasures. I know that stress cannot always be avoided, but I have worked hard to simplify and uncomplicate my life since the accident. I don't want to go through life on autopilot, as so many of us do. Do you know that I live in Arizona where we have the most beautiful skies? We have these amazing sunsets that I never took the time to watch. Watching them now brings me peace. They are so beautiful, and I like to think Davey is right there in the sun.

I have learned that I don't need a whole lot of material things anymore. My home is my happy place, and I have learned to be surrounded by the things I love as opposed to having the latest designs and furniture. Not that I could afford the finer things in life before! Those things just don't matter to me now. I've also learned that what is important to me is not necessarily what is important to anyone else, and that's okay. It's more important to be true to yourself, something I have had to learn the hard way.

I have learned that being bitter and angry over this loss does nobody any good. For me, the most important thing in my life now is honoring my kids—both of them. Cari needs me to be present, and Davey needs to rest in peace knowing that his mom finally got her s—— together. Somewhat.

I have learned and am reminded daily that life is precious and we are all vulnerable. Recently, my dad slipped on the ice in his driveway and hit his head. It was a very scary time for us, as he suffered a brain bleed as a result. He has completely recovered and is doing well, but it scared the crap out of me. This was yet another reminder that we really have no control over the big stuff. We have to continue to be present every day.

I have learned that I have a bit of a creative side. Who knew? I discovered during all this that I love making silk flower arrangements. I have never created anything in my life, let alone flower arrangements. I'm not even sure how I came about making them, but what I know is that I feel peaceful as they're coming together.

I have also started writing. I have always loved to write but never had anything that I really felt the need to write about before—until now. I started blogging after the accident as a way to cope with the pain. Now here I am, writing a book. It's something I hope to continue after this project is finished.

I still have days when I am overcome with the unfairness of it all. Why were we cheated out of a life with Davey? More importantly, why was he cheated out of his future? As I have said many times, there are no answers, and there never will be. And sometimes, that just pisses me off.

There are good days when I realize I have made real progress. When I told you I got a sickening feeling in my gut when I would hear one of his favorite songs? That is progress. Before, I would burst into tears and scream. See? Progress at its finest.

I worry sometimes too. Will I forget things about him? That terrifies me. The sound of his voice or his expressions. I have all his childhood memories all boxed up. I am still not able to open those boxes, but at least I know they are there. I have his pictures on my phone and computer. I've saved all his text messages on my phone. His Facebook and Instagram accounts are still active, as is his blog site. Some of his friends still check in on his page and say hello. I have pictures of him all over my house. I have his high school letterman jacket and his leather motorcycle jacket. I don't have all the things I wanted from the house, but I have my memories, and I hope they never fail me.

I miss him in a way that I can't properly explain. I am grateful that our relationship continues with him in the afterlife, but it's not the same. I will never again feel one of his big bear hugs. I will never again hear his laugh. I will never again see him roll his eyes at one of his sister's antics. I will never get another good-morning text just to see how I am doing. I will never again hear the excitement in his voice as he was telling me about work or the latest gadget he picked up for his car. I will never hold one of his babies in my arms. As hard as those things are for me, what kills me is that he will never again experience those things. That pain will be with me always.

Recently, Cari and I were talking about it being a new year. We are beginning another year without him. There is a lot to look forward to. Cari and John just got married, and they have purchased a beautiful new home in which to someday start a family. Rick and I are talking about what to do for our vacation this summer. We have recently done some work in our house that I am enjoying. It's such a place of peace for me. All these things are good things, but there will always be an element of sadness to them because of what we lost. I have become much better at keeping the sadness tucked away, but it's still there. We do have the joy of knowing that Davey is and will continue to be around us always, guiding us, loving us from afar, and encouraging us to follow our bliss.

About the Author

Debbie is a first-time author who felt compelled to write after losing her youngest child at age twenty-five from a car accident. Her wish is to offer some hope that other grieving parents can survive what is arguably one of the most difficult things in life.

Along with raising a family, she has worked in health care for many years. She is looking forward to the birth of her first grandchild later this year.

She lives in Prescott, Arizona, with her recently retired husband and fabulous golden retriever.

Lightning Source UK Ltd.
Milton Keynes UK
UKHW04f0612241018
331108UK00001B/75/P